the way of wonder

invitations and simple practices
for a vibrant life

PATTI PAGLIEI & JOHN SIMPSON

ROCK
POINT

Wisdom begins in wonder.

SOCRATES

Wondrous One:
In your hands,
however it got there,
you hold a piece
of our story,
ready to be rewritten,
in a way, by you.

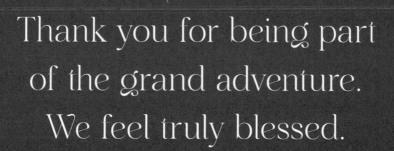

Thank you for being part
of the grand adventure.
We feel truly blessed.

CONTENTS

PART III: EXALTED ENCOUNTERS

PART IV: ONGOING CELEBRATIONS

INTRODUCTION

When we first received the invitation to write a book about wonder, it felt like a *way*. Could it be? We got together to explore if it was. If so, how might we go about writing it?

"We" is us three: me, my husband John, and my sister Lizanne. Together we had the good grace to cultivate Waxing Poetic from a creative instinct in my dining room back on Sycamore Avenue, in Los Angeles, into a wonder-infused jewelry company. We've touched many people with designs that celebrate being here together. Connections. Curiosity. Wildness. Personhood. Mystery. The love between us all.

We've been Waxing Poetic for just over twenty years. It has been a privilege. A lesson in living. A craft. We have consistently served up inspiration and talismans for our community—offerings of connection and openings to wonder.

So to be able to write *a book* about wonder, to have pages upon pages to explore the topic after working under its guidance for such a long time, is a serendipitous gift. We are as surprised as can be that this has happened.

This is how wonder works.

Over the years, our brand vision at Waxing Poetic has been to magnify the unabashed joy of living a vibrant life through poetry and stories that honor the gift of being here. This work is the basis of our book and the dawn of *The Way of Wonder.*

It is with a can-do zest that I have taken on the writing of this book as your solo narrator, but the concepts within it have been ideated, teased out, and edited with care through the extraordinary insights of my partner John.

In writing this book, I have had the cathartic pleasure of poring over the Waxing Poetic archive: twenty-plus years of poetry, fragments, prose, ideas, conversations, ramblings, and revelations—synthesizing some of our most moving concepts and messages and augmenting these with some new essays and insights.

But truly, the *way* of *The Way of Wonder* was uncovered through many late-night kitchen talks, wilderness walks, quiet understandings, and radical awakenings with John. We are co-creators of our life and this book. And co-experiencers. We've had our triumphs and thrills, but also trials. We have been through it. We've had significant losses and our dreams interrupted: my cancer, our daughter's illness, and many unforeseen life challenges. It is through all of these things that John and I can compassionately know anything about wonder at all.

Mostly, we know that wonder is an ever-present opening: a way of showing us how to move through life, so we don't lose ourselves. A way to save us from the tyranny of our heads on a moment-to-moment basis and bring us back into our life. The life we will regret not living later if we don't live it now. This is what we hope to articulate to you here.

I've separated the book into four sections: *The Invitation, Magical Gateways, Exalted Encounters,* and *Ongoing Celebrations. The Invitation* welcomes you to the possibility of vibrant living beyond knowing—the real freedom in life that we can have now. Each following section reveals where we might discover wonder (and how our life opens up when we do), through dedicated chapters containing a thought starter and personal essay. Each chapter ends with an invitation and a poem to help you keep wonder close as you voyage through life.

In the daily stress of living, it can be easy to forget to stop and sense the wonder of it all. The wonder of LIFE. Yet right now and always, even if we are caught up elsewhere, wonder is right in our laps, like a little, purring fuzzball, just waiting to be scratched behind the ears and tousled up to reveal itself in all its glory.

Throughout these pages, in some ways small and some vast, we uncover invitations to wonder that await with heart and intention for your journey. Some are easier and some more difficult, but all hold the same worthy promise: to imbue your experience of the world with all manner of goodness.

There is something so alive and magical about feeling the wonder inside and around you. It doesn't matter if you are lit by riding a wave, the darting of a hummingbird, a long shooting star, or a dull knife full of Dijon mustard. Get your wonder where you can. Like finding your balance on a bicycle, wonder will always set you right, show you what is possible, and whirl some wind through your hair while doing it.

John and I are not pretending we have this licked, but we know that this medicinal fountain is constantly flowing. And we want to help you (and ourselves, and everyone interested) to drink from it.

Welcome to **The Way of Wonder.**
We are grateful to be here with you.

John & Patti

PART I

THE
INVITATION

When you choose to travel life in the way of wonder, you see the world with less judgment and more possibility. Less knowing and more *wow!* The invitations are everywhere. Even if you're just performing a mundane chore, like washing the dishes, consider experiencing it through the lens of wonder. Washing that sink full of dishes may feel tedious, sure. Maybe even all the parts of the chore feel tedious. But YOU are not tedious.

On the contrary. You are full of wonder, surrounded by wonder, practically overflowing with wonder! And, when you access it, every suds-filled wipe of your sponge can be an ease-filled "take me away" moment (I mean, when was the last time you considered the miracle of soap? Sure, there is how it feels, how it was made, the bubbles, and how it cleans, but also: how it can wash your troubles away).

You already have your ticket to wonder. You might call it something else, but you have everything you need to gain access. We all do. So let yourself use it, let yourself look: The magic isn't as much in literally "seeing," but in making room for seeing more. For living more.

Unless there is some other reason, let's assume you came here to live. A most worthy endeavor! So why not make living your highest calling? Wonder is right there with you: to help you break through limited thinking so that you can honor the gift of being alive through the amazing miracles—and soul-enhancing choices—you're surrounded by all the time.

In part I, *The Invitation*, we extoll the virtues of this life we're charged with living and examine our current dilemma—the forces that constrain us. The mental habits that impede us from dancing with the wonder of life— all the brilliant, beautiful life—around us.

We each carry within us this great invitation: to live our fullest expression, to bring forth our gifts, and to return to our flow. Allow yourself to be fascinated to the core by the miracles around and within you. Your exhausted, overprocessing self will thank you!

Wonder isn't simply one invitation, but many, to the same glorious, coveted event: your life.

LIFE

THE GREAT AFFAIR

Life is magnificent.
(We really ought to pause
a little and *let ourselves*
feel what that means.)
Perhaps a bit of allegiance
is in order . . .

Ｉf you are holding this book, you are a part of *The Great Affair of Life*. Pause, dear friend, and take a breath.

Before we go on, please take a moment to feel life as it pulses through you and around you. Because, yes, you are a part of it—the whole of it, along with the rest of us—the spectacular, heartbreaking, ecstatic, salty-sweet, dazzling, tranquil, chaotic, trippy whole of life.

In this Great Affair.

In this Very Important Matter of Living.

We all want to live a good life. But there's always trouble accessing the good stuff in the face of all of the pressures stacked against us. We've been through a global pandemic and social upheaval. Economic uncertainty. We lost people we love. Our identity systems, beliefs, and judgments put us at odds with each other. Computers and technology have edged into the time that used to be devoted to neighbors and friends. What little breathing room we have now has been invaded by a "need" to thumb our way through served-up content on our phones.

If you are anything like me, you are hungry to find a more profound and nourishing path. You are no longer willing to live in a manner that betrays your deeper self. There is just too much at stake: our precious days are here, in this life, and beyond that lie our destinies.

While we have been busy looking elsewhere, making plans, and being lost in our projects and futures, wonder is (and always has been) waiting to turn us on. The good news is that we can always awaken to wonder and its endless possibilities.

As you may have already discovered, a more vibrant life is begging for attention. This is the idea that we are exploring in this book. We are so hungry for this soul fare: deeper, more resonant experiences. To get lost in the music. To transcend our trappings under a night sky. To liberate ourselves from dull, repetitive thoughts and actions. To experience and express freely, no matter what. To be here for all of it.

But what we're up against is a preconditioning to operate with efficiency: a relatively automated way of being that likes to recognize everything in the world by its handy label and move on. On a walk, maybe the internal dialogue on a good day when noticing a bird in a tree is:

Blue jay in the oak tree. It's breezy today.

Instead of seeing . . . just how acrobatic the maneuvers of the bird are as it weaves through the thick, shimmering foliage of the branches. As the breeze tugs upward, the leaves and branches of one group of trees after another sway madly. Loose leaves flying!

Maybe, *just maybe*, we outsmart ourselves. *Just perhaps,* we are missing out on being here on a deeper level. Indeed, we are missing lots of the vitality, connections, and wonder in life: the countless enriching experiences we've traded in so that we can keep up with the demands of our lives.

We have our problems, and we need solutions. And we want them ASAP. But while we seek answers, perhaps what we should be looking for is openings. This is to say, as Socrates first did, to examine our life.

To see past the quick labeling into the wonder
hiding in the slower reveal—if we can just pause to look.

To question our long-held beliefs. To dwell in a more humble way here, so that the amazing can blossom within us and all around us.

To embrace not knowing, and in doing so, initiate the way of wonder.

this mind-boggling life

On any given day, you will breathe in and out around twenty-two-thousand times. *Twenty-two-thousand times!* And you might go the whole day without being aware of even one of those precious breaths. On any given morning, as you lay here on the edge of a wild blue planet spinning in space, you roll out from beneath the star-filled darkness of night and into the light and warming heat of a gigantic ball of fire.

Just remember (on lots of occasions!) what a privileged trip you've set out on in this Great Affair of Life. Life on Earth is mind-boggling! We get to dance around in these incredible bodies (our space suits!) that allow us to thrive by breathing in what the trees and oceans are breathing out. Even if this whole thing is some kind of extremely persistent illusion, it's one heck of a show!

Surrounded by miracles that we often take for granted, it's so important that we pause and bask in the wonder of just being alive. Take a few moments to feel your breathing. Go outside and feel the warmth of the sun on your face and realize that the warmth is coming from a raging nuclear furnace some ninety-three-million miles away.

What an honor it is to be here together, alive on planet Earth.

While this life here might defy understanding, may we remember to pause in this glorious mystery and rejoice in being able to share in it.

Here, an invitation:

To envelop yourself in magic,

To move beyond the hard armor of yesterday

Through the invisible threshold

of another frontier

Up to this moment, you've held all the dancing:

all the night skies, all the yeses

There will be others, moments,

but in this light, in this season

There is grace, there is giving,

there is possibility

There is a new dawn rising,

there is courage to be celebrated

This gift to all hearts,

the light of a new beginning.

THOUGHT

MOVING BEYOND

The thing about thinking . . .
Such a blessing.
Such a trap.

Say you go to the beach on a lovely afternoon. It's more crowded than expected, so instead of feeling the soft sand between your toes and seeing the sun glint off the waves, you're focused on the crowds and your thoughts are consuming your time with a grinding, know-it-all tirade about *how it should not be so crowded with all of these people, it's never like this, blah blah blah . . .*

Getting out of the trap of our rigid, all-knowing minds shouldn't be such a struggle. The problem is that our trigger impulses to know and control things often get in the way of our more humble, not-knowing self that delights in discovery. When we are caught up in the clutches of our thoughts, we miss out on the constant wonder that awaits us. Our imagination and ability to see things in a new way get stifled.

We have been given an incredible privilege that separates us from the rest of the natural world: We can think—in very complex and abstract ways. Our far-reaching, progressive thoughts enable all sorts of breakthroughs. We have imagined and designed a way to put a man on the moon. We figured out how to break down a photo into an electrical stream of zeros and ones so that it magically floats from one handheld device to another through thin air. We have developed medicines and other lifesaving technologies. What a gift, these minds! But if we allow the powerful labeling machine of our brain to dominate our lives, our spirits are left malnourished and abused.

Wonder creates space for us to linger longer in what we don't know.

To experience the thrill of the question instead of rushing to accept the label and move along. To consider alternatives. When we throw out a question, we invite in imagination, and a new energy is created that lights up possibilities that otherwise wouldn't be there. Opening to wonder changes everything. Our energy becomes more gracious. We become more benevolent. Gentler. Wiser too.

This is who we are capable of being. This is the life we can inhabit. Anytime. Anywhere.

We get so much closer to the recognition of our deeper self if we can move beyond our already-knowing minds. And wonder helps. It can slow down our compulsive busyness. It can whisk us beyond rigid thought. It can give our richer life back to us.

Georgia O'Keeffe said something so beautiful:

> *"Nobody sees a flower really; it is so small. We haven't time,*
> *and to see takes time—like to have a friend takes time."*

Her paintings are meditations of a life well lived. They are beloved because they are offerings on the highest level of soul recognition. They explore the relationship between our inner and outer worlds in something so simple, and rarely really seen—a flower.

To truly see takes time. O'Keeffe found the time because this is what painting requires. Precious time, which our thoughts and the distractions of media and modern life threaten to steal from us. It is in the moment, the one that our thoughts so quickly move us away from, that we live. If we don't show up for our life, our busy minds will take over, and we may ask ourselves one day, "Have I really lived? Or squandered my time here?"

If we open ourselves to wonder, we won't feel as compelled to hold ourselves back from the incredible life we've been given. We will awaken to our higher calling and open the door to a life that can be imagined anew.

lighten your load

We cling to the tired stories we tell ourselves like clothes we've outgrown. And we carry them with us everywhere.

Our thoughts and judgments are the baggage we lay on ourselves and others. Let's set those down for a moment. They're just too heavy (and we don't need all that *stuff*).

We don't need piles and piles of outdated ideas. Shouldn't we make space to try on some new thoughts? So we can travel a little lighter? So we can go further?

A lot of us move through life with a load of assumptions, most of which are probably outdated. All of which keep us from experiencing life anew.

Examine each judgment as if it were a piece of clothing. Does it still fit? Even if it does, consider an update. Maybe, this time, try something a little different.

You deserve a few original observations. And if you want our opinion, light and fresh look good on you.

Don't let your dreams pass you by,
dear ones—

let them float long enough to notice,

appreciate, and speak to you.

A lot is revealed by the
cloud-watching observer's observations.

WONDER

THE SHIFT

Let the spark
that strikes your
as-yet-unimagined
fancy light a path of
small miracles.

Back to this gift we have, the invitation that is always in our pocket. Not a place or destination, really, but a *way*.

Be roused, dear one. This is exciting news! While this is not your typical invitation, it is as ordinary as the invitation to brush your teeth (with a smile!) each day.

It is . . .

A *serendipitous summons from somewhere* to transform any situation into one with more awe, depth, delight, and divine knowing.

An *energetic and encouraging epiphany* that reminds us that while life is emotional, heavy, and intense it is also beautiful, fun, and wildly delightful.

And it is all happening on this pinpoint of time. Right now.

No further explanation is necessary. And to accept the invitation, there is no RSVP required, and very little you need to do except this: You are (politely!) asked to quiet down and listen to life. Intimately and openly.

A momentous thing, but let's come together on this: There is no single way to get there because there is no there there. You just need to get *here*. And you can't do anything wrong. But you do have to show up, pay attention, and *feel*. If you find yourself doing this, you've made it. You will be here in your life.

Your presence at this great affair is welcome—here, now, always. Nothing is needed; just bring yourself.

Now that we are all up for living in the true abundance of life, we should do everything in our power not to miss out on it. So let's get down to it right here. How we experience the way of wonder—as less of a choice and more of a *shift*.

When I was in art school, I had a passionate painting professor who instructed us to squint when we looked at our work. To engage in the act of seeing in a new way. I took to this practice wholeheartedly. I'd squint, lay down a few brushstrokes, squint again, and paint some more. Eventually, after much trial and error, my painting style became less methodical. I began to access something more profound in myself through the work, which became more joyful. The work was better, as was I—as both a painter and a person.

Wonder is the metaphorical squint. It is the finer lens that lets you see more deeply and clearly what is in front of you. When you use it over and over, you will appear. You will return to yourself and all the richness of this big, beautiful life. This is where you will discover the awe-inspiring creative act of the masterpiece you are composing.

Forgive me if this "your life is a masterpiece" business sounds daunting, but all worthy endeavors are. And you are worthy of this endeavor. Embrace it. If you don't know what to do, remember, the brush is in your hand. But also remember, you can put it down for a bit. And squint a little.

Wonder doesn't dull or deaden you. It is not a set of expectations and instructions.

It is here to open your mind to infinite possibility

through your widened imagination and sense of perception

in the ever-present living moment.

There is no destination to get to, and no big decisions are required. Just explore where your life is flowing and where it may be off. Be on the alert for what turns you on. Know that you have been gifted a good foundation.

Let yourself shift as often as necessary. Take risks, push through your constraints, and let yourself get wild with living.

allow

On the glorious trip of life, we may certainly encounter obstacles, but fortunately, wonder is here to help us navigate through them . . . even to find presence and joy in them.

But first, we need to loosen up. Because trying to control the uncontrollable is exhausting, and there is an easier way.

Picture yourself in a boat on a river. You've got the oars in your hand, and you are rowing. You are trying to steer toward someplace you thought you wanted to go, but the current is against you, and it is getting dangerous. So you drop the oars. You let the waters carry you for a while, to a peaceful part of the river, where you find relief from working so hard.

Ah, relief.

To receive its gifts, life only asks that we touch it. Lightly. Conflict will still arise. But remember, you can drop the oars. You can shift. *Easy does it.* You will make it, and you will be better than okay—you will be changed.

Remember this when you are struggling to control things: relax instead. Allow. Let life happen.

Let the rising and sinking of the sun

Be a lyric

Let the moon and the tides be a phrase

Let the stars be both signs and tiny songs

Let a child explain the universe—

And for the telling, let it be true,

let it be an anthem

To love and life and letting go.

PART II

MAGICAL GATEWAYS

There are many entry points to wonder. Not all of them are of the stargazing variety, though.

Sometimes, we are brought to wonder's gate through no choice of our own: a difficult diagnosis, a disability we struggle with, a breakup, a trauma, a loss that sets us off on an unintentional journey.

While we don't choose these difficult experiences, we can choose how we move through them and allow them to touch us. One of my own dark passages was when I received a cancer diagnosis. I would never have chosen this for myself in a million years, but it was the beginning of a radical transformation that I don't think I would have achieved without passing through the eye of that needle.

Our challenges can be so intense, yet also so generative and revealing. Helping us to wake up in the now, they humble us and empower us to go deeper. However unwelcome, however uncontrollable the situation is, it can be a calling to find meaning there and to transform ourselves.

We find light in all our trials and losses. As a lantern reveals the hidden in a sightless landscape, so does wonder show us the way. This is the significance of the dark. Like stars that can only be seen in the night, the darkness uncovers the otherwise hidden.

In part II, *Magical Gateways*, we visit some of the challenging places we are sure to face in our time here on Earth—the hard parts inherent in humanness: difficulty, fear, doubt, loss, courage, illness, and darkness. We explore each of these challenges as a "gateway" of inquiry—a portal to deeper connections with Spirit and purpose. The *Magical Gateways*: *magical* because of their supernatural power, and *gateways* because they are intimately human passages that lead us within.

And as we pass through each gateway, we uncover this gift—the thing we are called to trust: the light that senses we are there. The one that illuminates this achingly wild, sacred, beautiful life.

DIFFICULTY

THE RUT

Nobody likes
a rut.
Except, perhaps,
a seed.

Let's start in one of the most feared, difficult of places. *The rut.*

Rut, defined:

"a habit or pattern of behavior
that has become dull and unproductive
but is hard to change."

A seemingly stagnant place, no?

Yes. And, most relievedly, one of the many playgrounds of wonder.

Are you stuck in one of those *waiting-around-in-the-dark-seeking-light* places? So was once the seed. Are you feeling a little unclear about things? The seed was too. Willing to surrender the former image of yourself to explode with new verdant life? You'd better say yes, or wonder will prod you with a generous spurt of hose water until you do.

Okay, maybe the notion of being a tiny hard seed in a dank situation offers no hope. Full of potential but treading in muddy water, the seed must risk the death of all it has ever known for a future of uncertainty. Yes, that is a little scary. But through the lens of wonder, it is more a miracle.

The seed emerges tender and victorious from the depth in which it was planted. It accepts the light of the sun and grows the strong, inherent dream that is its destiny. Somehow, quite miraculously, finding ourselves in a rut implores us humans to do the same. To begin.

So yes, feeling stuck is sometimes not the trap it seems.

Not at all. Sometimes, it's a niche that has been readied just for you: to explore, curl up in, reach out from, and then burst up and bloom through.

If you should find yourself in a rut, then, befriend it. Ask it questions like,

"What am I doing here?"
"Where else should I be?" and
"What good is it to protect this dull shell of familiarity?"

Visit a garden, real or metaphorical, for proof. Seep into the moment. Experience it as the death-cracking, life-giving space that it is. Let it widen. Leave behind the hardness of knowing everything already. Soften. Feel your way. Open yourself to the beauty of what you may take for granted in your everyday life. Feel the expanse of your world. Of you.

I know that the ruts you might find yourself in are deep. Dark and frightening too. Yet by the time you realize you are in one, you're already on the path to awakening—to the unknown possibilities and your individual potential. You needn't let extreme hardship be the only way you come to this. Just as every challenging place is a gateway to the wonder of transformation, so is each moment. It is here, now, asking us to pause, be brave, and be willing. To be a seed.

A rut invites us to grow. It is an opening to seek, touch down into, and explore. To rest and percolate in. Not on our own, as the mind would lead us believe, but instead in the vital sureness of the earth, of life itself.

grow

You may ask, "How?" As in, "how do I make a change, a life, a difference?"

How do you?

This lovely French phrase may help:

Vouloir, c'est pouvoir.

Literally,

"To want to is to be able to."

Simply, *want* to. Then, *do*.

See also: start. See also: begin. See also: become. See also: act. But first? Start.

How?

Ask a question. Listen for clues. Ask for help if and when you need it (and you always need it, so always ask). Consider some way other than the one you already know.

Start with what you have: an idea. A wish. A hope. A belief. A stubborn disposition. And no second-guessing—you have what you need, and you need to act and act now.

Remember the seed that awoke from the dark rut to burst forth and grow?

It was able to.

And so can you.

Love letter to a seed:

You are safe here

(wherever that is, no matter how hidden)

You are loved now and always

You are stronger than you think

You are far from lost

You are splendid

You are capable

You are alive

You are not even close to stuck

You are loved and this means

You are free

Always and forever,

Your companion in life,

The Rut.

FEAR

RISK & RECEIVE

Risk and receive:
Brave one,
The world rejoices at
your revelations.

During childhood, on some level, we were conditioned out of taking risks. Usually, because we hurt or embarrassed ourselves, or got shamed for doing something. Or because someone told us what we wanted to do was wrong, shameful, or would hurt us or someone else.

Fast-forward to now. We're adults with jobs, houses, cars, families, and such. With all these things, and grown-up expectations put upon us, we find ourselves taking even fewer risks because we feel like we have more to lose. So it's no surprise that for many of us, our childlike hunger for life, and our dreams, have both ended up on the shelf.

The supposed safety we aspire to is quite attractive, but it isn't real. For the most part, everything can be ripped to shreds at a moment's notice. An expanding life isn't about playing it safe, but rather living it.

And lots of the best bits of living are found through the gateway of risk.

Think about it: When you were born, you moved from the comfort of the womb to the unknown world outside. Take that as a warm-up lesson for all the glorious living you will want to do throughout your life. Get the heck out of your comfort zone and come alive!

Like every other person, you've experienced challenges. Likely you've been traumatized by something, and perhaps disappointed by much. You've been scared, you've sacrificed, you've witnessed suffering, and you've suffered yourself. You've had your heart broken and felt pain. You may even have been taken to the edge by illness and cancer, as I have. Look at all we're capable of surviving.

Life is an inherently risky business. And I know it is hard sometimes. But it's when we move through our fears that we feel exhilaration and gain valuable experience.

That said, how often do you quickly write off taking a risk? Your auto-response is, "No effing way." What if you could slow down that snap judgment? Take a couple of breaths and ponder what great things might be waiting for you if you let yourself be vulnerable enough to take the chance. Could this give you an opportunity to try something new that could change your life?

First of all, your life has already changed just by opening yourself up to the possibility of taking that risk. Now, if you sit with it a beat or two longer and say, "What the heck?!" instead of "No effing way!" your life is now really alive.

Your willingness to let go of automatic, safe (boring) responses has revitalized you. A new spark is at play. An act of willful defiance against those fears and doubts creates energy!

Once you break from inaction, magic happens.

Instead of fearing the spark—the risk you must take to cross into a new frontier—you can let it empower you. As you stand up to your fear, you engage in a world of discovery. Of course, you don't always succeed, but one thing's for sure: You miss 100 percent of the shots that you don't take. And if you don't take those risks, how on earth can wonder, waiting for you on the other side of risk, blow your mind?

Ask anyone who has achieved any meaningful growth in their life. Just as our pasts can victimize and disable us, when we choose to be present wonder can unfold to enable, encourage, and strengthen us.

Victories await when we trust the shift from knowing (knowing that it is a *very bad idea*) to embracing the unlimited possibilities that live abundantly in the unknown.

 Take a risk

Here's the thing—when you contemplate doing something and you hear that auto-response of *No way! That's too risky!* try answering with something like this: *Bing Bing Bing! There must be gold in them hills! This deserves closer inspection.*

Allow yourself to move forward. Find out for yourself. Feel the thrill in real time.

Some risks are not worth taking, but so many possibilities are shuttered because of knee-jerk reactions. And if it is something that you love and feel compelled to do, however terrifying, well, you might really be missing out.

Whether it is taking a risk on another person, a new endeavor, spilling a hard truth, or pursuing something you've always wanted to do, you will be blessed in ways that you will never have known had you listened to that autoresponder in your head.

Tease it out. Dance with it. Take the next step.

Shimmer and shine

Your starry self is something worth sharing

Show your splendor

In deed or in delight or in doing right by heart

By love and wonder

By all that is true and good

By believing in risk

And knowing

Even when and often how it's hard

That we will make a better world

Together bit by bit

And bright starry self by

Bright star.

DOUBT

THE
WELLSPRING

Do not be afraid
to take a detour.
You are not lost.
You are finding.

*D*oubt is a doorway. Please don't get stuck in it.

In the early years of Waxing Poetic, I was in full flow. I had designed an innovative product and cultivated a brand that stood for meaning and expression with a great name (thank you, John). With my sister Lizanne, we launched into a market where it just exploded.

Success! It was this entrepreneur's dream.

But soon, with business booming, things got "real." Employees, inventories, deadlines, consumerism, PR, pressure, money, marketing, decisions, opinions, etc. As the founder, I was excited to expand my mission. But as the CEO, I was challenged. The feeling was close to something like a well-meaning but naive hippie chanting for peace in an overcrowded shopping mall.

In my transition from dreamer to delegator, my office went from a bright yellow funky studio loft to a bland box in a corporate park. From designing whatever I wanted to what the market dictated. And as an artist/designer-turned-executive, my new responsibilities were often at odds with my creative intuition.

I had a vision that others thought was brilliant, but I was feeling hollow. I wanted to build a great company, but I was frustrated. I needed help. An internal battle took control while I kept smiling and blindly following what the other people I had surrounded myself with told me to do.

My self-doubt-driven internal monologue went something like this: *I am just an artist, after all, a designer. What do I know about running a company? I'd better hire coaches, consultants, advisors, and even astrologers to help me. I'm exhausted. No, I'm fine. Really.*

Doubt had shrouded my light. And though it appeared that others seemed to doubt my own leadership, I see now that I was the doubtful one. At times, I believed my colleagues more than myself. And if I questioned my leadership, how could I blame others who believed the message of "not enough" that I was sending?

The truth is, I was enough. Enough to be the leader I could be.

Still am. But never the leader I thought others expected me to be. I was performing, and I lost the only voice I could ever try to lead with: my own. And soon cancer came.

When I sought post-recovery treatment from a naturopath, she asked me how the years had gone before cancer. I cried when I told her how I had struggled.

"Cancer cells are undifferentiated," she said. "They don't know their purpose; they just multiply and grow for no reason."

They just grow for no reason because they don't know why they exist?

I listened deeply.

How could I have let this happen? Was I not awake? Are we all somewhat asleep? I was so foreign to myself back then. A construct of a leader. In a construct of a business. In a world of relentless productivity. My life had fallen out of purpose, and my business and I both became sick. I could not turn away from the truth that arose that day. And I knew I needed to work the muscle enough to live it. And I would. By cultivating a deep trust in myself, I eventually overcame the need to look for answers outside of myself. My whole life opened up because of this, and our brand became much stronger because of it.

These days, I know what real nourishment feels like. And I seek it. And I hope you do too. And to each of you who is reading this, I hope you can know with some level of certainty that you have it inside of you.

You have a wellspring that can float you through the doorway of doubt, without hesitation, into a new, stronger conviction of self. To find this unwavering wonder, look no further than within, and you'll discover a continual supply of true self-confidence, held in the bountiful source of your infinite spirit.

Doubt, especially self-doubt, really seems to relish its insidious and ruinous role as it spouts up: "What!? You can't do that! You don't know how to do that!"

And bango—the action is halted, your confidence bleeds out, and you are stopped dead in your tracks.

But . . . when clearly recognized for the shyster role that doubt often plays, it's truly a neon-lit gateway to wonder. Because when you say "Whatever!" to doubt and forge ahead to do the thing that doubt says you cannot do, you will do just fine and love the accomplishment (and what you learn by doing) even more.

So when you hear that BS artist telling you how or why you shouldn't do something—for any number of reasons that it fabricates for you—see it as a glaring invitation to trust the process and forge ahead. The wonder is in the doing, not in the not-doing. The knowledge will come to you as you move ahead.

If you don't think you have what it takes, let the wonder in yourself strike a line through that:

~~DOUBT~~

Now, DO honor that arsenal of gifts you have so generously been given. DO take action. DO allow yourself to figure it out. Trust that you can DO it. You really can.

Sometimes,
doubt is to be expected,
allowed even,
given a brief audience
Once in a while
But to be doubtful too often
Is to shut the door on wonder
To be too filled with something
other than light
other than love
So set it down, breathe it out
look inwards
or homewards, or upwards
yes upwards
the stars, darlings, are our distant cousins
reminding us
of all the glow within ourselves
that we are charged by.

LOSS

LIBERATING LIGHT

Beloveds, remember:
No one we love,
and nothing we love,
ever really vanishes.

Last summer, while my mom lay in hospice, I was scheduled to go on a long-delayed vacation to France with my family. To say I was anxious about leaving wouldn't quite get it right. I was more afraid. Deeply so, in the heart way.

Mom had been slipping away from us for some time, the ravages of dementia and congestive heart failure slowly closing down her human form. She was thin, increasingly confused, no longer able to get out of bed, and barely able to talk.

The week before I left for my trip, I spent several days with her, as I'd done every month since she'd become bedridden. We'd eat together, clink our wineglasses *To Life!*, go on conversational adventures, and maybe she'd remember a thing or two, and we'd laugh. It felt like sacred grace to be at her bedside. I was grateful that she was in no pain, yet it troubled me to leave her. It always did, but this time was different. I'd be out of the country, and she'd be farther away.

I explained to her that our family would finally be taking the trip to France that we had postponed for years. That John and I would take our daughter Lulu to see the Eiffel Tower in Paris and meet up with friends at a wine-country château. That we were all looking forward to it.

She couldn't always understand everything anymore, but she understood this:

I was having a hard time going.

"GO." She made it very clear that I not only ought to go, but then, in words that took her a few seconds to conjure, she whispered in a singsong, animated, sparkly breath, "WONDERFUL. Do it while you can."

During that visit, as always, I asked mom, "How are you feeling?" This time, she transmitted a sense of peace and said plainly, "It doesn't hurt." Her soul smiled, and a brightness in her being sought my own. It was then that I came unshackled from my fear of losing her.

It was the surprising glow of a beginning. A possibility. A liberating light.

The deep sadness I felt while leaving her was still there. But for the first time since she had been sick, there was also an embrace of completeness. As I pressed my lips onto her forehead, I didn't know whether I'd ever see her in this form again. But my heart knew that we would never truly be separated from one another.

So, I made it to France. One day, after walking the grounds at Rocamadour, I was drawn to the dimly lit chapel. In the center, the Black Madonna emanated a powerful presence. To the left, a chorus of church votive flames waved peacefully.

All those lives, I thought—all that light.

A comforting stillness enveloped me. It guided my hand as I lit a candle for Mom. *She would love it here.* I opened my eyes. There was a soft light pulsing from the devotion-blue glass. Without any thought, I kneeled.

The tender luminosity that filled the space was love itself.

When I returned from France, I went to see Mom. With every "How are you feeling, Mom?" her answer, reliably coming from her spirit, not her body, was, "I feel good!" What we both beheld at her bedside was love itself.

Each time I visited, there was space and freedom, despite the unknown that was ahead for each of us. Mom showed me the way and, in illuminating it, the answer to my most pressing questions: there is love, only love.

AN INVITATION TO . . .

remember

Take care to remember this: despite fear and darkness, despite worry, despite grief, despite apparent-seeming absence—

Despite all that is illusory, the unnecessary phantoms, the fallout of someone forgetting that above, under, over, beyond—and in all of us—is infinite, immortal love—

Remember you are part of it, that love.

Remember your beloveds are too, now and ever and always.

Love has no endpoint but is a continuum: a place to know and be known. A place, but also a way: endlessly accessible through presence.

Despite location changes or what feels like chasms of loss, love is present. Just as a cloud manifests from the ocean, and returns to the atmosphere as rain or snow, every manifestation of love, each beloved, is always with us.

It is in this wonder where we rest from sorrow. Where we are always known to one another, and to love itself. Where we remember and are comforted by truth.

It is an unplanned dance this time
sometimes
with elements of transformation
and loss

But we are and will be, and always have been
capable of and fortified by hope

The heart to open, the heart to see
that beautiful indefinite

Always here,
Love is always with us
As is will
As is wonder.

COURAGE

SET THE TRUTH FREE

Courage is not
a measurable thing
in scale or weight
but instead by
and via heart.

Our daughter Lulu has struggled with outbursts at school. The other students and most of her teachers didn't know until recently that she had a large brain bleed when she was six years old, and it took two brain surgeries to fix the problem.

In the years following, she had setbacks. I remember when she first got home; upon seeing a bowl of strawberries, Lulu said, "I don't know what these are." She had trouble with many of the things that used to come easily—like remembering the alphabet and writing her letters. Even locating the bathroom. So much had to be relearned. But eventually, she did. And along the way, to help her get by, she developed a wickedly smart and compassionate sense of humor, one of her most distinctive traits.

Now that you know we've got a funny one on our hands, the part of her story I'd like to share with you (with her blessing!) is a tender moment of wonder.

After Lulu had an impulsive episode on the first night of the big class field trip earlier this year, John and I were called and asked to retrieve her. A couple of days later, the three of us met with the head of school while the rest of the class was still away. Lulu was encouraged that day by this insightful educator to stand up in front of her seventh-grade class and share her story—what she'd been through. The secret she'd been keeping. It would take a lot of courage to do so.

Lulu probably doesn't think of herself as courageous. Honesty usually comes easily for her. But this was different. She feared that she'd be judged for sharing what had happened to her. All kids at this age need to be accepted in their friend groups. She was afraid they might not like her anymore and that it might open her up to teasing.

The night before she addressed the class, we worked on what she would say. But after a few minutes of trying to help her, she shut us down. "Mom, Dad—I got this." She was the only one who could do this.

The following day, as they approached the school, John asked Lu, "So, how do you think this is going to go?" Lu paused thoughtfully and just answered, "I don't know."

The assembly was scheduled to happen in the afternoon after lunch. Then I got this email midmorning (her exact words): "So it turns out instead of later today im talking about my surgery now. i love u ill email you about how it goes. extremely unexcited. my stomach is turning."

After school, the calls came. The kids told their parents what had happened, and each of the parents called to let me know what a positive thing Lulu had done—that Lulu stood up and told the class about her surgeries and that she was still recovering. That she spoke about how it was hard for her to restrain her impulsive outbursts, but that she is working on it and that she asked for their understanding and support. How, amidst tears and high fives from the students and teachers, she had set her truth free and welcomed compassion and healing for everyone.

If we genuinely want to live, we can't hide. We must risk being hurt or embarrassing ourselves. But here is the amazing thing (and where the wonder is):

When we tell the truth, we make it safer for ourselves
and others to be who they are.

We generate possibilities greater than our judging minds would otherwise allow. When we step into truth and overcome fear, we summon the courage to live with integrity and release ourselves, and others, into freedom.

So fight this hardest battle, and never stop. Don't hide. There is great wonder for all in just being who you are.

be seen

Our favorite definition of courage is one found in the *Oxford English Dictionary*:

Courage: the heart as the seat of feeling, thought, etc.;

spirit, mind, disposition, nature.

The heart. Yours. It can be many things. When you speak up for yourself and what you believe in, or stand up for others, it will shine as a heart of service. This is what you are armed with—your powerful, courageous spirit.

There is no more marvelous thing than just being yourself. So, use the most significant expression of who you are, and that heart of yours, to do the things that scare you most. Tap into what you feel you must do—that if you don't, part of you will remain hidden—and unchain some truth, your spirit.

Love yourself fiercely enough to do what you need to do. Come into your own, and be seen.

You are courageous.

Armed with a luminous heart,

Afloat and adventuring in
this universe of miracles,

Gifted with the openness to love
and love onward

To welcome the Divine
in one another and yourself

To make room for wonder

To welcome uncanny connections

To be known and curious and seen.

ILLNESS

THE NUB

Be brave,
be bright,
be brilliant,
be wild.
Roses have managed
it for centuries.
So can we.

Consider this: What might need to change? Or even go (however painful) so that a greater potential can emerge?

Here's a little story to illustrate this consideration. The concept of *The Nub* was introduced to me by my dear friend and fellow breast cancer survivor Kyra, who used the metaphor to describe what it was like to go through treatment.

"You sorta feel like a nub of yourself," she said, describing the indescribable.

Kyra looked as radiant to me during her treatment as she ever had. And though her already thin body had been made even slighter, her shaved head was covered in a bandana, and her usual energy was drained, I remember the distinct feeling that she was clearly in the midst of something life changing: that beyond her illness, beneath the surface, something much deeper was going on. She looked different, and she'd been through something scary, yes. But she was still there—and by this, I mean her powerful presence. Seeing her stripped down in that state was like witnessing the force of divine potential itself—the impulse to live beaming through so clearly, despite all that was taken from her.

The Nub. The most essential part. The part that stays when all else is taken or falls away.

After I recovered from my own breast cancer treatment, Kyra and I celebrated with a couple glasses of wine. We shared our chemo-chair stories, our hair-falling-out stories, our who-is-that-person-in-the-mirror stories. And when I told Kyra I thought she was spot on with her nub metaphor—that there pretty much wasn't a better way for me to describe what I had become during treatment—we knowingly shared a laugh. It was a kind of spirit laugh. A beautiful, aching laugh, the kind that touches you deep to your bones.

Here we were, each of us on the other side of cancer—more fully present, grateful as all hell, and not taking for granted that we survived. Releasing it all—essence to essence, nub to nub.

A few sips from saying goodbye, our once-numb-from-treatment fingertips held glasses that clinked a toast to each other.

We are still here, my friend.

Yes, we are. So alive in our profound connection to each other. We were now free from the illness, yet present to discord that ultimately opened each of us up to truly living, despite the difficult stuff that we had to endure to save ourselves.

Like Kyra, I didn't see my cancer coming. And when it did, though it hurt hard, the gift of it hit loudly too, forever turning up the volume on how beautiful and sacred this life is. Before cancer, I used to listen to my screaming fears and worries, but now this symphony of vibrant breath and bountiful life that I am blessed to have has drowned all that out.

We are so much more than our bodies and circumstances. Our essence is life itself. When I see others going through an illness, I think about this—how a person can look depleted or perhaps feels like a nub of themselves, but their entirety is in there.

John often tells people how I came back from cancer stronger than ever. He tells friends he got a new, more alive wife—thirsty for adventure and living!

While I would never wish for anyone to get cancer, I would encourage you to meditate on the lesson of *The Nub*. To uncover that essential part of yourself—the nub of you—by exploring what you might have to let go of. To gain wisdom in the process of looking at your life choices and discarding what isn't true for you. To trust nature and the power within you.

When something is taken from you, it is a loss for sure. But here, wonder is waiting to arise like a rose to unfurl some promised new beauty—releasing you into a new acceptance and understanding, a different way of being. It will give you an intimacy with your life force, new insight into your struggles, and help you move beyond fear. Though not always easy, wonder provides ease and expansion, so that you may blossom onward, and be spectacularly alive.

AN INVITATION TO . . .

thrive

Seasons, feelings, and flora change—all things are transformed.

Consider this: In every season, even the coldest and darkest, there are flowers blooming somewhere—promising the observer that change is constant, reliable, and transformative. And promising that life wills itself to continue, even amidst great odds.

Just as a rose changes, from bud to blossom to glorious spectacle to something other, it is beautiful still. Even when the bloom is off the rose, there is wonder waiting.

Observe a flower. Let it remind you of your own potential for healing, your own potential for greatness. For rebirth too.

Be reminded that blooming is an act of will. And resolve. Trust that we all can bloom onward, at any stage. And ought to.

Be mindful of the tiny, darling.

Buds start out tightly wound
but bloom bright

Stretch out your expectations
like branches

and unfurl your bold heart.

THE PRISM OF POTENTIAL

Bright hopes,
bright ideas,
bright dreams,
bright beacons.

These are the things,
You bring to the world.

To examine why darkness is such an important gateway of wonder, let's look at light. Light as in air. Light as in flight. Light as in color.

Light as in . . . butterflies.

Swallowtails, morphos, monarchs. I love all species of butterflies. You probably do too, if you love having your mind blown by the path nature has set them on, their beauty, and their triumphant changes.

We all appreciate the butterfly as a long-regarded symbol of transformation, evolution, and new beginnings. These miraculous creatures have fluttered their way into many of my designs because of this, their natural impulse— their act of literal transcendence from cocooned form to flying wondrous creature. They are so captivating because they awaken us to the necessary process of metamorphosis in such a gorgeous way, alighting us to our own beautiful becomings.

But what often goes unappreciated about butterflies is how much time they spend in darkness, in the pupa—or rather, the chrysalis—which is a most beautiful word for a very dark passage that our friends must go through on their journey to realize their wings.

In its form as a hungry caterpillar, this magical creature stuffs itself with leaves, sheds its skin, and spins a silky cocoon around itself in darkness like a magic act. What is going on there?

Usually, the emergent winged butterfly gets all the glory, for it represents victory, transcendence, and beauty. But what about the dark, mysterious cocoon? So again, what is going on there?

A not-so-random guess: radical transformation.

The caterpillar is called inward, and it disconnects. Then, it consumes itself— its old form—to free its earthbound self. To become "beautiful" and fly. The wonder in this act is the butterfly, but the way of wonder here that is so overlooked—where all the real action and transfiguration happens—is in the chrysalis. The dark cocoon where the former self lets go—in a way, "dies"—so that its life force can reach maturity.

Eventually, the butterfly escapes its confines, shirks off debris, and then . . . ascends!

Just like how a glorious awe-inspiring rainbow forms when the sun breaks through the rain clouds, there are conditions that must be met for a miracle like this to occur. For the butterfly, the condition is first to be a caterpillar, which is called to trust its mysterious, innate natural process and hang in the dark for a while.

And it does—in a terrific way that should be honored as the brave act it is. In the absence of shame or blame, the butterfly-disguised-as-caterpillar does what it must do to refine itself: to spin into darkness, go inside out (literally!), and form all over again in the most magnificent image of its true potential.

It is only through dying to its caterpillar image that the butterfly can emerge to embody the color and magic it's meant to bring to this planet.

Now with wise wings of wonder, this exquisite creature

can seek new grounds and flora, miraculously able

to see things from a different vantage point.

Gloriously able to do what it formerly could never do. Fly.

When we are shut down, compelled to retreat, feeling strange and not at all like ourselves . . . when it is hard to see and feel and know what comes next—we can remember the caterpillar. How it welcomes its dark down period and trusts that its day will come.

emerge

So much life happens on this Earth. But think for a moment about *where* the Earth happens—amidst the darkness.

The beautiful blue ball that sustains us and every other living thing is a vibrant occurrence in a profoundly dark and infinite space. Our Earth. Each day she spins around the sun, delivering on her promise to draw us from the darkness. But what is our promise to her?

Every morning, when we wake from the darkness of night to the light, we are called to participate. To emerge.

First: Swaddle your heart, and hibernate if you wish. None of this spells doom, brave one. You have been given everything you need to be safe while you grow. Give yourself time. When you are ready, feel your wings.

When you are even more ready, emerge. Notice how you've changed. Now, make real change. Every chance you get.

Rainbows don't so much come
Out of nowhere
As out of the present's potential,
For while there are dark clouds
And sometimes formidable showers
A rainstorm is also a symphony
Of individual droplets
Of individual instances
Each with the potential to reflect and refract light
Each with a weight and purpose
Each and all important . . .
And when conditions are right
And we pause and let ourselves notice
. . . the rainbow, the actual rainbow—
We are, if only for that moment, transformed forever
So it is also with love
So it is also with life.

PART III

EXALTED
ENCOUNTERS

Fundamental truths do not need grand entrances to be knowable or seen, but just some attention (namely, ours) because they were here and true and potent before we ever noticed. These are the ordinary and also unexpected miracles that occur in our daily lives. Even in an empty room, we are surrounded by these wonders in waiting.

These are the *exalted encounters*, where we can enact wonder in real time. They are not instances or occurrences that happen under certain conditions. These are encounters, meaning something unexpected we come face-to-face with: the chance meetings and unplanned shifts into wonder. They are always here, like air. And they are exalted, because they are on the highest order, and bring us immense joy.

These are often the "aha" moments in life, but also more silent revelations that invite presence. Sparks, both gentle and great. Epiphanies, along the lines of *I never noticed . . . I think I'm in love . . . This must be happening for a reason . . . I had this feeling today . . . I was moved . . . Last night I realized . . .* And some can't be articulated at all, only felt.

Exalted encounters don't announce themselves. They wait quietly for us to open so that we may receive them. They can be wooed with our attention, but can't be forced. Often, they seem to just show up. Mostly, exalted encounters hang in the air like sweet anticipation, waiting for us to bump into them, stumble upon them, notice them, and invite them in. Seems that when we open up to wonder, they start happening.

In part III, *Exalted Encounters*, we explore the everyday miracles of the ordinary, the phenomenon of alchemy, and the accidental gifts of serendipity. We uncover the expansive life that is available to us in the "now" and in the unknown. And we illuminate how things start working out when we listen to our intuition and use our facility of seeing as a deep way to experience life.

These marvelous ways of wonder are quite unexplainable. To the mind, that is. But to the awakened heart and connected spirit, these encounters are a homecoming that only need be felt.

THE ORDINARY
LIFE IS DELICIOUS

Sometimes it is the familiar
that shifts with fresh eyes
and becomes otherworldly;
the natural becomes known
and then unknown
An unfurling of secrets
And deep joy, beaming
across a vista both
homelike and new.

And now, dear ones: something wonderful and yet entirely familiar to ponder. Magical and beautiful, just like you.

Apples.

Life can be so delicious, no? Yes! But we forget this sometimes: that paradise really is portable, and within reach. It's as close as an apple in your hand.

One bite and you're . . .

. . . *besotted*.

You thought I'd say doomed? Like Snow White? No. Not a chance. Because while this world is a wonderland, it is not a fairy tale. And while a bite of that poisoned apple caused Snow White to fall into a death-like sleep, she was eventually kissed awake by true love (insert your own idea of the kiss-giver "person charming" here). That was one powerful apple. But that is just a story. And this here is real life.

And apples are real. *Extraordinarily so*, says wonder.

Yet while they are very, very real, it does remain true that apples are fraught with symbolism, both old and new. Not just as a storied, mystical, and forbidden fruit, but also as a symbol of youth, beauty, love, and happiness. See also: immortality, joy, and transformation.

See also: exalted encounter.

See also: wonder-hiding-in-plain-sight.

See also: delightful disruptor.

See also: see.

To really see an apple as the marvel it is. That sounds woo-woo. But who cares? Living is at stake here. And we don't really see as deeply as we should, not always, and not just apples. We don't always play in the realm of ordinary marvels, and we are missing so much because we've been conditioned out of taking the time to be with life in this way. Out of noticing the radiant gifts that are here for us, not to be experienced with our achieving minds, but with our hearts instead.

So, wonder reminds us of this dynamic: When we seek beauty in the ordinary, we become present to readily available treasure. Treasure that is just waiting to be discovered and then shared.

A life that is here and now. Delicious life.

Let yourself come alive in the ordinary and discover what comes next. It might start with an apple, and then you get the impulse to share. To create. To play a little. To take care of yourself by taking a break.

Maybe you gather more apples, gorgeous organic apples, and in quiet reverence, you make some pie. It is a beautiful pie, made with intention. And lots of butter and cinnamon.

And you share it. This life-giving pie. The smell of goodness. Delight that money can't buy. You've broken from the to-dos. And a celebration ensues.

Bite by bite, true communion unfolds. A sense of delight emerges as you reconnect with what has gone unnoticed. And there is love present, and health, and kinship. Togetherness. Your very alive heart recognizes the beloved life it has been searching for. All this potential is held in the ordinary apple. Fruit of the tree indeed.

make room for marvels

Life calls us to be unabashedly present. How do we make this happen? Start. Really, decide to do it. Decide to be present.

Begin by making room for ordinary marvels. Some room in your mind, in your day, in your overall goings-on: to allow for the unexpected appreciation of the ordinary to emerge.

Think about the fairy dust quality of a child's spilled glitter mishap, for example. Take a moment to watch the sparkles float. Laugh with the child instead of running for a vacuum because, in that little space, you share some magic. You make an example of finding delight amidst the confusion. You celebrate something ineffable.

Take a moment to notice what is right in front of you, anything, with all of your senses. What does it look like, smell like, feel like, taste like?

Make room for marvels.

They are hiding in plain sight. And when things get messy—and they always do—try to go with it. Marvels could be hiding in the dust, needing only to be given a little bit of room to show themselves.

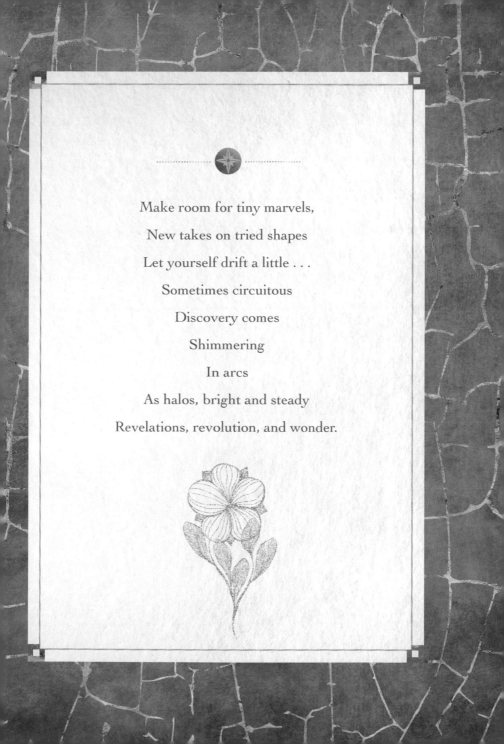

Make room for tiny marvels,

New takes on tried shapes

Let yourself drift a little . . .

Sometimes circuitous

Discovery comes

Shimmering

In arcs

As halos, bright and steady

Revelations, revolution, and wonder.

THE GOLDEN PRACTICE

Love is all the things
we cannot name
but that save us
with regularity.

Before there was what we understand now as chemistry, there was alchemy. People were working in caves and dark rooms and basements and labs, trying with all their might to mix elements together in the hope that they could make gold. It didn't work. They failed . . . at gold. But what they were able to accomplish left more than enough record for the next round of scientists to pick up and use. And lo, chemistry was born.

However, alchemy didn't vanish. It became something else. A word to describe a process that is so effective, so transformative, it seems like magic. Alchemy comes close to the spirit of trying, believing, and wanting very much for something to BE, and throwing oneself or the efforts of one's heart all the way in, with the belief that perhaps something better will happen.

Arguably, love is a kind of alchemy.

Love—the practice of love, the actions of giving and making room for and extending oneself and sharing resources to make more love—is itself a kind of gold. But more than that, it is *a golden practice.*

All of us have been transformed by love. As much, also, as we transform ourselves through love. Consider great love stories throughout the ages and our own encounters, and there will be one thing in common: that love usually brings people together in an almost magical way.

In the wonder space of love, there might sometimes also be an unnerving sense of possibility—a twinkle of anxiety about how we show up for these encounters and where they will go. But when we remind ourselves that love is both "everything" for us all, as well as a malleable array of tangible actions, intentions, risks, and rewards, we're at least on the right track.

It is by risk and openhearted exploration that we seek to create a kind of love between us and the other, whoever that might be. And possibly, it should be given to *everyone.*

In her wonderful book *All About Love*, bell hooks wrote, "A generous heart is always open, always ready to receive our going and coming. In the midst of such love, we need never fear abandonment. This is the most precious gift that true love offers: the experience of knowing that we always belong."

If we can even approximate a modicum of that sense of belonging and perfect place, of safety and warmth and acceptance with anyone at all, if even for a few minutes, then we are doing the right thing.

> *Love is our very best, most fail-safe homing device.*
> *Love is also home.*
> *Love calls us home to ourselves,*
> *makes us home, and sets us free.*

Love is the thing we are making—and making room for—every day. Love is what holds us together, what makes our hearts sing, what lights up our faces, what induces impromptu dance parties, what electrifies Zoom calls, and what makes us pause and stare awestruck at the person we're about to give a present to (because if not for them, if not for love, all we'd be holding is a pretty object).

Eternal, bright and saving, love can never really vanish and always reappears in wondrous ways. It is what holds us together. It is all of us.

Love is why we are here.

AN INVITATION TO . . .

love

In *The Glass Menagerie*, American poet and playwright Tennessee Williams writes that time "is the longest distance between two places." While there is evidence to suggest that at least in some situations this can feel inescapably true, we're offering an additional consideration: if time is the longest distance between two places, then love is the shortest.

Perhaps even going further than that, we're of the belief that love has no distance, but instead by its very nature, attributes, and potential, it transcends distance. Love is simply the shortest, smallest, most efficient miraculous thread that ties all of us together.

So seek the tie of love, and let it pull you. Let it catch and carry and bind and bear you. Let it unravel you. Let it tether you to the safety of your own—or another's—heart.

Be pulled together in love. Let it lift you up and give us all the lift we need to gather the good within ourselves and all around us, so that we may form bonds and be set free.

Remember: love is something you do, but more importantly, it is something you can become.

Love ignites,

as does longing,

as do wishes,

as well as

so-close-you-can-almost-taste-them,

as-yet-unrealized imaginings.

SERENDIPITY

LET THE UNIVERSE WORK

A gift,
a miraculous
accident,
An entry point
to more . . .

Sometimes it takes going out on a limb to find out that the universe has our backs. I'd like to share a story that John told me about how he learned this lesson firsthand.

When he was twenty-nine, he embarked on a solo surf trip through Central America in a Volkswagen van. When he arrived in San Jose, Costa Rica, a day after Christmas, he made an "I'm alive and well" phone call back to the States.

After the call, John was watching a parade pass through downtown. A random, red-haired man on the crowded sidewalk caught his eye; he had the sense that he knew this stranger. John felt like he should talk to him, but the man slipped off into the crowd. A little while later, the stranger reappeared next to John and started a conversation.

The man's name was David, and though he was living in San Jose, he was from California. David was impressed that John had driven solo all the way from Los Angeles, but when he learned that John's VW camper was parked around the corner, he told him matter-of-factly that it had been broken into and everything was stolen. John was in disbelief— he'd parked there the day before with no issue. But unfortunately, when they got to the van, he saw that David was right. John's stereo, guitar, cameras, tools, and most everything of value were gone.

David liked the van and gave John his number, telling him that if he wanted to sell it, to give him a call.

The next day, while surfing, John suffered a debilitating injury. With intense pain radiating down his left arm, he struggled his way back to San Jose to find a doctor. He had herniated a disc in his neck, and the doctor advised that he fly back to the U.S. for proper treatment ASAP.

Since there was no way John could make the drive in his condition, David's phone number felt like a godsend. They got together later that day and began trying to locate an attorney to process the required paperwork for the sale, but lawyers were impossible to find during the Christmas holidays. Without this paperwork, John would not be allowed to legally leave the country unless he drove out in his van; he needed it to prove that the 100 percent luxury tax on the sale of the van would not go unpaid by the buyer. Waking in pain in David's driveway for the fifth straight morning, John approached David and asked him to just drive to the airport with him to see, if somehow, he could get out without the paperwork.

When John entered the terminal, he approached the first airport employee he could find and explained his predicament.

"No problema," John recalled the man said, "go buy your ticket."

Full of blind trust and ecstatic, John jogged back to his van, took David's $4,000, and bid him adios. After John purchased his ticket, the airport employee reappeared. He pointed John in the direction of a woman wearing purple in Passport Control. John swears that she winked at him before she stamped his passport. When he saw the helpful employee again, he nearly hugged him. He thanked him profusely and gave him a hundred-dollar bill. John said he was experiencing the worst pain of his life and was never more relieved to return home.

Always confident and capable in his adventures, John usually needs very little help. But this time, he did. And it showed up like magic.

In a larger sense, the universe worked, supporting him in serendipitous ways behind the scenes in his time of need.

The same ways of wonder can work for anyone willing to trust and give the universe a chance.

Trust the universe

Give the universe the opportunity to show off how it can work for you. This can be a little tricky because if you don't step into the unknown without a safety net, you may never know how the universe might help you. But if you push the limits some, you'll find out.

This is a trust exercise. Like falling backward into someone's arms, you need to let down your guard, and trust. Trust the universe. Let it surprise you. Let it catch you.

It is such a wonder when the universe flexes, demonstrating that it all works out in some mysterious way. And when it does, be humbled. And emboldened. Trust more deeply in our miraculous, intelligent, and connected world. It's got your back.

Just say it—*the universe works for me.* Say it all the time.

Surrender to the light

that you cannot catch,

the parts you cannot see,

but the wonder you can feel.

NOW

A
SWEEPING
REALIZATION

All hail
periphery moments
and
threshold spaces.

Something occurred to me the other day while I was vacuum-sweeping the kitchen floor. I was wielding what, in my house, we jokingly refer to as my "domestic goddess wand," which makes this particular chore that I despise not only bearable but also fun (I didn't know I had it in me to keep such a clean kitchen, thank you very much, Dyson).

I'd just come back from my daughter's school, where they had held a parent coffee gathering. Since I was gone for most of the morning, I was happy to be home, so that I could return to the writing of this book.

I usually write in the morning, fresh from waking up, when I feel the magic in the air. But this time, it was midday, and I was behind schedule.

Fully intent on getting to my writing, I dropped my bag. Then, the stack of mail in my hand led me to the counter. The compost bucket was sitting there and needed to be emptied, so I did that. Back with a dirty bucket, I went to the sink to clean it.

Then, the Ziploc bags called—we never throw them out but cleaning them is a job I wouldn't say I like more than vacuuming. Once the bags were cleaned inside and out, I did a 180 to the kitchen island, where we'd missed some Italian bread crusties the night before. My mind returned to reality. As I moved my laptop, I brushed the counter with an anxiously annoyed swoop of my hand. Down to the floor, a few crumbs dropped.

I must clean this floor, and I must do it NOW.

I grabbed the Dyson from its hanger on the garage wall and dutifully reentered the kitchen. Alone in the house with just the dirt and my thoughts, I swept away. Particle by particle, much was illuminated on the floor by the otherworldly green light: dust and dog hair, crumbs, potato chip pieces, a clump of oatmeal Lulu had dropped when taking her bowl to the sink that morning.

Slowly sweeping, also, my thoughts.

I need to be on social media. But no, I don't. Do I?

Sweep. Keep sweeping.

The Metaverse. Will that really become a thing? No, go away, Metaverse thought; you annoy me.

Sweep, sweep, sweep.

What if Lulu is hiding something from me? No, she isn't. But they say most kids her age do. Should we start a parent group to talk about these things?

And keep sweeping.

One last swoop under the table, and before I knew it, I was done. Twenty minutes felt like five. The floor was clean, and it became clear: as I meditatively moved through the seeming chore of sweeping the floor, I had swept myself into a series of *nows*.

As in any meditation, when you settle in, thoughts arise. The "seeing" self that is at the seat of our being observes our compulsive thoughts and gently whisks them away, revealing presence itself. This is what it felt like, though how it happened took me by surprise. My act of sweeping—more, and longer than I intended to—wasn't a sitting meditation, but it got me out of my head just the same. I'd been caught up in thoughts of the future that I wasn't even aware I was thinking. As I silently swept, a presence arose in me that brought me back from the stressful clutches of anxiety that I was feeling.

When it was over, like upon waking in the morning, I barely knew I was gone. I hung up my domestic goddess wand and sat down to write. I was as receptive and open to the wonder of my experience as if I had started fresh in the morning.

Some might call my cleaning detour procrastination. But what I had accessed—first unconsciously, then with great consciousness (and a rush of peace)—was the opening of aliveness.

Available in every moment. My life. The Now.

get out of your head

There is always an indisputable sense of something close to (if not actually) magic that hangs in the air, awaiting your presence.

It is Now.

And it is ready and waiting for you to drop in. To welcome you with a spacious, ever-expansive hug. To offer you peace and relief.

It is your life, where it happens, truly. *Now.*

Your mind will remind you that you may have been elsewhere or need to be elsewhere. That you haven't done all the right things, and that there is uncertainty remaining. The Now is inviting you to get out of that confusing place. Because there is somewhere else you belong.

In freedom. Which is *Now.*

Now, bring your intentional awareness to what you are doing at this moment. At any moment. If you find yourself stressed, suffering, lost, tense, overwhelmed, or anything at all.

Drop into NOW.

Insight and liberation are so, so close.

Sometimes we need a small gesture,

or a few

Something sweeping, to remind:

that each of us,

in our own way,

is a chance for peace.

THE UNKNOWN

WHERE LIFE SHOWS ITSELF

In the wild,
in your beautiful heart,
in your precious
(yes this one) life,
your wings are shining
and you are free.

We lose a sense of control when we embark into the unknown, and it can feel scary. We have to pay much more attention when we're not sure how things will go, and it's more work for sure. But it's in taking those steps into the unknown that life can show its stuff.

We exist in a time where most of us live in an overabundance of comforts compared to our ancestors. Leaving comforts behind and embarking into the unknown lights up questions like:

What if? Do I have the chops?

Fortunately, it also lights up generations of seekers and survivors who got us here, who still live deep inside us all. And if you listen hard, you'll hear their response:

Only one way to find out.

One weekend, a couple of years ago, my family and I headed out to Santa Cruz Island on our boat. We made the hour-long crossing escorted by pods of dolphins that jumped from our wake. Because we got a late start, other boaters had already tucked into all our favorite anchorages. So, we started exploring.

With a couple of hours of daylight left, we motored beneath the dark and dramatic cliffs towering over the island's northwest end until we could peek out toward Santa Rosa, the next island in the chain. Also ahead lay the dreaded "potato patch." We had no plan for that. It could be super tricky to cross the middle part of the channel between the two islands where it can be nasty with chop and multidirectional currents. Plus, the anchorages on Rosa are much more exposed.

But this day, we had the perfect conditions and enough fuel and food to wander over. We were screaming—

not a *Here goes nothing,*

but a *Here we go!*

We dropped our anchor into the sandy bottom of a beautiful, expansive bay. There was not another soul in sight. We plunged into the light blue waters, our daughter Lulu egging us on to *cowabunga!* from the roof of the pilot house.

Soon John and I were making margaritas and cooking up a lovely dinner of steak, sautéed onions and mushrooms, and spaghetti. At the same time, Lulu danced back and forth between the two stand-up paddle boards that dangled off the stern, falling in repeatedly, squealing and laughing.

Our boat's not big. We do all our cooking, eating, and general hanging out in the open air. And when you get a rare windless night, as we had, it's a reward to be out on the belly of the calm sea under the huge star-filled sky, especially with the moon-drenched beaches and rolling hills of Santa Rosa Island wrapping around you.

Thankfully, the night remained calm. In the morning, we paddled onto a new frontier—our black sand beach. In all of our stays on Santa Cruz Island, we'd never experienced a beach anything as remarkable as this. We explored little caves and found beautiful rocks and shells. John and Lulu smeared the black sand—which sparkled like magical fairy dust—all over their faces and bodies.

Then, so inspired, I took a stick and wrote in the sand,

When you fail to plan, you plan to live!

We felt like the only human beings on Earth, roaming the island and swimming in the blue waters like the free people we were born to be.

get wild

Following all the rules and remaining close to the comforts of home can feel nice, but it's doing absolutely nothing to liven up your primal senses and energy. Just the opposite. When's the last time you cut loose?

If you need some encouragement from an authority, I'll lend you some inspiration from our pastor. Not his exact words, it came across something like this—*God gave us our wildness for a reason. Celebrate it! Don't hide it. It's a gift!*

Whoa. I wish I'd heard this message when I was much younger. It always seemed to me that instructions from "on high" were to stifle wilder instincts. And whenever I unleashed my wild side, I'd be sure to serve up a nice side of Guilt to go along with it (just to be cool with the big guy). So to have our pastor advise us to celebrate our wild side, I was like—*Wow! I agree! Finally!*

So—go AWOL. Get off-piste. Let your hair down. Give your wild self some wild space to come alive. I know you need it! We all do. Desperately.

Let's run into the wild, shall we?

We think yes.

Surrender, just a little. Do.

Shoes off, hair askew,

And all your beautiful selves aswirl . . .

The adventure is never the same twice.

INTUITION

LISTEN TO YOUR WHISPER

Never underestimate
the power of your heart
as both a compass
and a teacher.

It was at the Rose Bowl flea market in Pasadena. Amidst a tray of tchotchkes, I found some random brass stamps—the kind people used in the days of letters to make wax seals—in different styles and shapes. A voice inside nudged me: *You need these.* That was all the information I was given.

So, I bought a few and took them home, where they'd sit in my dining room studio on a tray of vintage jewelry treasures I'd collected for the hand-beaded jewelry designs I was doing back then. I figured someday, maybe, I'd do something with them. Not long after, I was on the hunt in an antique store I frequented. I came across the antique seals again, this time a complete set. I'd never seen them there before. A feeling arose in me, dancing up my spine to the base of my head. Then, *whoosh!*

I held the stamp collection in my hands, a complete box (all twenty-six of them!) as if it were a newborn baby. My heart's guidance pulled me so hard I must have looked possessed. That's sure how it felt. My eyes scanned the shop as if someone could peer into my brain and discover what I'd just been given. As quick as the idea came, so did my internal voice, shocked at this epiphany.

Has anyone not done this yet?

My palms were tingling right to my fingertips. I really couldn't believe the transmission I was receiving that day in the small antique shop.

Could I do this?

I didn't give myself much, if any, time to think. I just raced home to find out. I stamped out the alphabet using wax sticks I bought at the art supply store, with the goal of having them cast as sterling silver charms. The impression of each letter in the wax was perfectly imperfect. Just like us—the people those initials would represent.

How this idea came about can only be described as a divine chain of events—entirely orchestrated by intuition and acted upon by impulse (aka, listening to my whisper . . .).

There are those stamps again,

followed by

You've gotta take these home.

It all started by tapping into something that felt familiar to me—meaningful, original, a little wonky, and out there. But it was the synchronistic series of events that brought the thrill—and me—just outside my comfort zone (where we know all the good stuff happens). It was here that the idea that would sustain me—and a company—was born. And then, there was John's epiphany at the dinner table,

We should call these Waxing Poetic.

And then, the kismet via my sparkly, helpful showroom manager,

I know someone in Bali who can cast these . . .

And finally, my sister Lizanne's insight to place the product in the gift market (where it was a massive success) . . .

Waxing Poetic is a gift!

Opportunity doesn't always announce itself. Sometimes, it blows at the hairs on your neck in whispers. It draws you to something you don't quite understand yet.

I've never figured out why or where the voice comes from. But I have learned to obey it. Because as much as I have benefited from listening to my whisper—what my gut tells me—I have also made major mistakes by not tuning into it. Severe. So if I may, as someone who has done it both ways—and is also an off-the-chart Myers-Briggs "I" (Intuit)—

Trust yourself, please, please, please. There is magic here. You don't need much more than this. Listen to your whisper. It is there for a reason.

follow your heart

We are so often swayed by what we "think" we should do. Jobs or vocations that don't quite feel like us. Some way of living or being that doesn't align with who we really are. We go through the motions and look for guidance. We wait for something to light us up.

A bit of inspiration, if you will. Some wonder.

Enter, your intuition. The single most helpful navigating tool we have in this life. It is that sense, a pull of sorts. A calm, inner knowing.

It is trying to reach us, but it can also be sought. We just have to tune in to where the aliveness is in us.

Things are always very clear in the heart. And in the body. So, listen for clues. Don't think; just follow the tingles.

It is not an answer but a way.

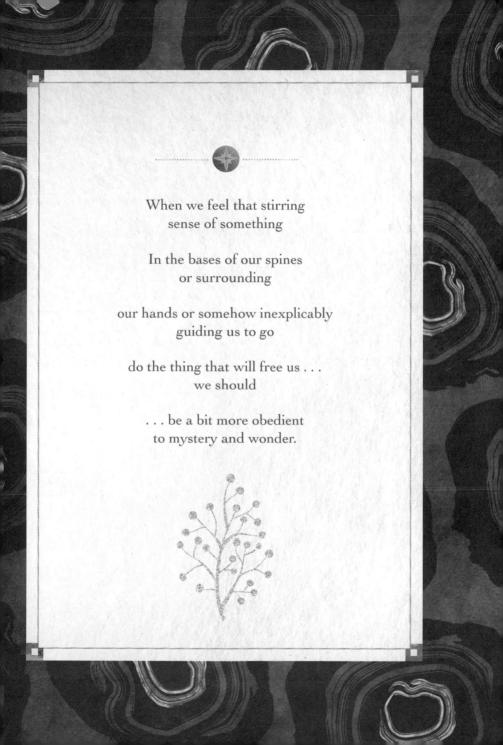

When we feel that stirring
sense of something

In the bases of our spines
or surrounding

our hands or somehow inexplicably
guiding us to go

do the thing that will free us . . .
we should

. . . be a bit more obedient
to mystery and wonder.

SEEING

THE CACTUS FLOWER

Think about this:
All of those moments
when the Divine decides
not so much to drop by,
but instead it is you
who decides to
take notice.

On my morning walks during my chemotherapy treatment, when I felt particularly weak, I would say hello to the cactus blooms along the way, always inspired by the beauty that springs from such a seemingly inhospitable plant. Astounding beauty. And surprisingly so much more to her than what met my eye. Before cancer, I was too distracted and busy to have a chance encounter like this.

I was looking for you,

I would imagine the cactus flower calling me.

And I, you.

Many days, it felt like the miracle of the cactus flower kept me going. My encounters with her always left me tingling as the world swirled on my little street, coming alive like a Van Gogh painting. I'd come alive too, the brushstrokes in my body inseparable from those of the world around me as I'd float home with my precious life force powerfully charged.

I'd taken many walks in my mornings and had never before experienced a cactus flower (or ANY flower) in such a profound way like this. The truth is, life was waiting for me to slow down to a stop and take notice. The dark side of that truth is: it took a life-threatening illness to slow me down enough to see.

I have never been here the same way since.

Often, when we are aligned with life, coincidence presents itself. In this story, it is the connective energy in the humble cactus flower. It is something I innately felt then, but I gained some proof in my research. One of the most powerful things the cactus symbolizes is the ability to see beyond what is visible with our naked eyes.

To see beyond what is visible.

There is so much more we can realize than our eyes can see. This way of seeing—not of the mind, but of the spirit—is a way of wonder. It is exemplified in the infinite life I saw in the little flower.

My exalted encounters with the cactus flower so moved me that I designed a small collection inspired by her for Waxing Poetic. I never wanted to forget how this delicate-yet-strong life force—a survivor like myself—revealed herself to me, bursting forth with presence, showing me my own.

When the collection was released, I shared its origin story. So many people felt as I did—moved and maybe even cracked open a little by it.

Years from my healing and magical rendezvous with the cactus flower, I still let myself notice her everywhere.

> *When I get lost, I look for her—*
> *she, who is always looking for me—*
> *the one who dwells in me.*

The beautiful cactus flower. What a miracle she is. That her essence was once hidden inside the rigid and hollow cactus, in a barren place, in an extreme of life, where against the odds, she sought the nutrients she needed. That she sprang from such hardship.

That she even exists at all.

How her tender blooms are protected by the cactus needles . . . how we can all soften in the light. So many mysteries held inside. Our hearts are not so different.

see deeper

Wonder invites you to be ever more aware and awake in the world, your surroundings, and your reality. As a start, can you trust (for a moment) that the benevolent universe and the Divine are aware of you too?

Welcome the full dimension of your life, just beyond your conscious mind, looking to meet your gaze.

Every moment holds a mirror: not for future planning or past reflections, but rather to *see through*. Use it to access your boundless, more connected spirit and discover a world full of color, healing, and horizons unknown.

Walk lightly, and welcome wonder. Notice the aliveness around you that is also vibrantly within you. Realize your wholeness and belonging. Your profound and gentle awakenings quietly await, ready to demonstrate to the heart what is not visible to the eye.

Accept the invitation to *see deeper*.

Now think about this,

How we want to pay attention

How there is always a new way to see

How you can always look deeper.

PART IV

ONGOING
CELEBRATIONS

Be reminded that life isn't as scripted as it might appear, and even if it seems otherwise, no one is stopping you from rewriting it.

We want to celebrate life. When we celebrate something, in the literal sense of the word, we mark a place in time with shared significance; we make the thing celebrated more meaningful. We celebrate as in enact, celebrate as in participate, celebrate as in listen, learn, share, and receive tiny transformations.

A celebration is both an event and an action. We chose the term *celebrations* because we want to engage in the enjoyable activity of being here together. But also because when we esteem life and show up for its celebration, we realize that we are the most important guests of honor. And when we celebrate life, it's *ongoing*—ongoing celebrations. They typically move us out of ourselves into the world. They are new beginnings, improvisational discoveries, and the fleeting joys and deep transformations we are rewarded with along the way. We cannot be alienated here, even when alone. We cannot be absent from life when we are this joyfully engaged in it.

A child who has yet to learn limitations or judgments is in an ongoing celebration. Joy comes easily to them. They find magic in the simplest of things. They have these great imaginations. They access wonder so easily. They are little wonders!

In this final part, *Ongoing Celebrations*, this is what we want to get back to— the simple wonders of life. So that what might feel diminished or empty in us may be filled back up again, where we release our strains and remember our song.

It is a great sense of belonging: to joyfully attend our unexpected triumphs, the somewhat victories, and the silly but significant moments. To be present to our shifts in perception and changing directions.

It is a way: the one that guides us off the worn-out course. The one that leads us home.

THE STRAWBERRY MOON

Cartography of
a different kind
renders life like a globe.
As if one could ever
navigate your heart.
Wrapped in the path
of the moon,
and probable stars.

It was a warm June night in Santa Barbara. John, Lulu, and I met our close friend and her son for dinner. I had recently finished chemo, and we were seated outside. I could almost smell the sweet aroma of the summer solstice.

Something about the sparkle in everyone that night made everything seem more. More connected. More authentic. More excited to be together. It felt hypnotic. Crisp rosé, warm chips, and guacamole never tasted better.

A colossal moon lit our table. Our friend told us she was anticipating this particular "supermoon," which happened to be the last full moon of spring and the first full moon as we entered summer. That evening was a special one for sure.

An ecstatic aliveness arose in me. A softness was illuminated.

Above our stories, there she floated, beyond beautiful.

My soul lifted and seemed to leave me for the sky. Gone from the conversation, and I—pardon me—was drawn to chase it. I was out there somewhere, in the oneness. Then back to the scene at our table, a realization. A pale champagne-pink type of glow . . .

How rare this moment is.

I was in a place in time with people I loved. A moment that will never come again. Lit by an extraordinary moon.

And so are we. Rare and remarkable.

Just like that moon, every moon, every moment.

The feeling I didn't want to forget could never be captured. Not really. But the designer in me wanted to try. I imagined a piece of jewelry—a spinner pendant I called "Moongazer." The symbolic front was a champagne-pink crystal-faced moon. The wake-up call on the back: "Rare."

I later discovered that the particular name of the brilliant moon I had communed with was "Strawberry Moon." It originated with the Algonquin Native American tribe in the northeastern United States and eastern Canada and referred to the region's strawberry harvesting season. Not the moon's hue at all. Or any other mystery she held. "Strawberry" was simply her name for a brief period of time. Not describing her essence or how she made anyone feel. So much more than her label, she glowed a color all her own. An infinite story, like us, always in progress. Never the same twice.

To have such an intense revelation under the Strawberry Moon that night made me realize how often we are not having revelations.

Sometimes it's that we are just getting swept along in life. We're products of years of Darwinian evolution, after all. We've got things to do. Yet we are half awake. We get things done, yet are restless for wonder. We succumb to easy distractions instead (scrolling; things like that). We live much of our lives in our heads, even when there is a big, beaming mystery glowing in the sky above us.

Our habits seem normal. But, as we know, nothing *seems* like what it really is.

We have one precious life here. And it's up to us to set some excitement in motion, so that we can bump ourselves out of that half slumber. To let our souls loose and our spirits fly a little.

To drift in each rare scene in our life, precisely to come home
to the thrilling mystery of who we are.

When we can't do this ourselves, our blessed universe helps. It might be a difficulty that slows us down so we can recalibrate. A chance encounter that startles us out of our "meh" and into our majesty. Or, in this case, something that shines an ample light on life's mystery, that makes us go, *Whoa.* Something that happens once in a Strawberry Moon.

AN INVITATION TO . . .

each rare occasion

Sometimes we think a good life is about the "big" events—those dramatic full moon moments. But the moon is always a rare mystery, whether she is shining, a sliver, or hidden. And so is each and every happening in our lives.

"The question is not what you look at, but what you see," Henry David Thoreau wrote. You can create excitement in your life just by bringing your attention and love to something. So why not see everything you do as an opportunity to fire up your life then? Even a mundane event can be elevated to extraordinary when you give it your focus and reverence. So do.

To begin, reframe a moment as a rare occasion (because they all are, or can all be). See the moment as so. Meet it with your attention, and animate it. Let yourself go a little crazy now: maybe you plan a new moon polar bear plunge with a pal, make a collage of cupcakes to celebrate Wednesday, or forage a wildflower and herb bouquet for a friend. Or just go all a-buzz in glorious solitude. Accept everything around you as fodder for occasion-making.

Create your own new wide-eyed language for living an ecstatic, everyday life just by listening, seeing, and making it so.

Hold close, darling—everything:

this place, this scene,

these beautiful characters . . .

As the moment slides away,

another draws in

Another

Oh. Yes.

Another

This. Miracle.

WANDERING

THE MOVEMENT IS YOURS

Now is your
story season,
your sauntering season,
your slow-down-and-
look longer season.

We are often overwhelmed by external input in our daily routines. How do we give ourselves a chance to break free and discover what mystifies that inner light of ours?

The answer I'm about to lay down for you here has been a nonnegotiable for me on my own path of healing, fullness, and self-discovery, and I hope it will be for you too:

Wander within yourself. On purpose.

Yes, my beautiful, responsible friend, it is time to *take a break from your busy schedule to celebrate yourself.* I know this is HARD. It's hard for me as well. I get it—you have so much going on, right? But soon, you have a couple of days free, you say? And you have a vacation scheduled somewhere in the future, and you'll find time for yourself then?

Planned escapes are great (who doesn't love a getaway?), but the "celebration of yourself" that I'm proposing is a more common occurrence, meant to disrupt your daily routine (and even take over a bit of it). Wonder would like to give you permission to wander, to be ambushed by the longing inside of you, and to follow its lead.

Perhaps you surrender to the inexplicable pull of a side street (the air smells like jasmine! Someone is playing the trumpet! People are laughing in a musical language!). Or you stop en route to somewhere else to smell an exquisite ballet-skirt-worthy peony (one that requires wandering off the path and several yards into the possibly overgrown garden). Or maybe you are compelled to duck into an antique store for no express reason or to hike that trail that twists and turns until you find a magical glen, or . . . (if you are used to wandering, you know there is no end to the "or" options here, so I'll stop).

How do you feel when you let yourself go? I'd guess that you feel alive. Maybe even a little ecstatic.

Because when you wander, you listen to yourself. This is thrilling! You awaken to the guide inside. You stumble upon Something New. You are alive in the brightest sense. And in the joy of letting go, of following your heart and instincts, you gain valuable perspective that stays with you and becomes part of your operating system.

Wonder suggests that by way of this exalted method of musing, mirroring, meandering, and then (yes!) living, not only do you unmute your inner muse, but you also move beyond wandering alone, contributing to a creative arc of connected aliveness that involves a menagerie of people, places, precious moments, and perfect peculiarities.

There is an expression "wend your way," which doesn't get used often anymore, but I think it should, particularly because the word *wend* is wonderful. *Wend* comes from the old Germanic root word *wand*, the same word where *wander* comes from—whose meanings include (all at once) to turn, to twist, to consider, and to transform—rather like making a path or a life.

We should never underestimate or take for granted
how the course of our lives can change entirely, beautifully,
and boldly by the simplest encounter.

And it does not require us to follow one established map or a singular set of directions. Just to honor our impulse to slow down a little and free that part of ourselves longing to be felt.

The good Earth and its people here provide us with plenty of experiences, but it is when you wander that you are drawn to the movement that provokes the experience. That movement, beloveds, is yours. It is the celebration of your life, and in it, *all* of life.

AN INVITATION TO . . .

find new freedom

It can be easier to stay in our routine than to escape it when responsibility overrides spirit. But we rediscover hidden dimensions of ourselves—parts of ourselves that have been longing for some airtime—in the unexpected. Wonder desperately wants to show us this freedom so that we may live a fulfilling and meaningful life.

Lucky for us all, we each have the capability to break from constraints, even for a small while. To slow down and let our minds (and bodies) wander off-piste. To bring some calming clarity amidst confusion. To explore, ponder, and reconnect with what really turns us on. To just see what good feeling might await there.

So ask yourself,

Where in my life can I use some new freedom?

This is a good place to start. And,

What part of myself have I been ignoring?

Let this neglected part of yourself guide you.

Wander and find out what is here for you, right now. Normalize the sense of freedom you feel. Say yes to the invitation to celebrate yourself, every chance you get (or create).

A sort of spice in the air
A quivering of wind
Connections abound for
A well-nourished spirit
About to embark on
Another endeavor

Dreaming leads to waking
And waking leads to doing
Something leads us here
Our hearts are nearly quaking
For adventure to appear.

PLAY THE NEXT NOTE

Take a breath.
Let life back in
between
every
little
hurried
thing.

Improvisation spawns wonder, and as a musician, John seems to always find the most energy and joy when improvising—all ears and exploration. Whether he's solo at the piano or jamming with others—making it up as he goes along—that's where he says the thrill lives for him. I'd like to tell you the story of when John first fell in love with playing piano to encapsulate this idea of wonder and improvisation.

He was a sophomore in high school, and he and his best friend snuck into the school chapel where a grand piano sat under the tall, concrete arches. When he sat down on the piano bench, a creak echoed through the cavernous space. He said he struck a single key near the middle of the keyboard and held it.

John recalls how he and his friend sat and listened to the sound of that one note with a shared sense of awe that lasted until the note's energy faded. He said that one note thrilled them both so much that he played another note and held it. He and his friend listened and looked at each other, astonished by the beauty of that sound.

Two notes played together followed. Then three in a row. It went like that.

Not knowing what the next note would sound like, not a word was spoken.

He remembers that their hearts were just filling with something so simply beautiful.

As wannabe musicians, John said they felt like they were both getting in on some secret. The indescribable depth of the reverberant tones, and the endless way that a keyboard—even with no sheet music to follow—could be played to open the heart and touch the soul.

It is the wonder of the beginner's mind. Being with something as if it were for the very first time. Not knowing what note or chord is coming next. Not knowing what words or phrases will bubble up in the broth. A sweet, unrushed relationship with the subject at hand. Being open to it. Seeing it. Hearing it.

Improvisation leads us to creative beginnings.

When we let go of having to be experts at something or needing results of some kind, we can experience moments as they are. We can discover something new. And who doesn't want more discovery and *life?* Let yourself approach moments with inventive, awe-seeking eagerness. Whether you are reaching out to strike one note on a piano, for a spice jar in your kitchen, or to touch the shoulder of a friend: if you are stuck in some preconception of how it should go, you'll never discover what could be.

make it fresh

Oftentimes the mind offers up an auto-torrent of ideas. They can seem brilliant, yes. But, we can't possibly act on everything that comes to us, nor should we. Instead, we can divert this influx of ideas by seeing them as a sign to create an intentional interval—some breathing space.

Ah.

Because to intentionally slow down and wait, to let a pregnant pause hold the space between words, between steps, between notes—this is a whole other thing. Especially in these busy days when responses in conversations are so often in rapid-fire delivery to compete with the myriad of things demanding our attention; especially in a culture that has us programmed with behaviors that have not worked out so well for us: pauses provide critical space where we can create something entirely new.

So take a respite. Have a conversation where you pause for a couple of breaths, even between words. This shift should work like medicine for the busy mind. Slowing like this can lead to the ultimate wonderous realization of "I am." And, if so, there you are.

Just try it. Pause before uttering a word or note. Surprise yourself and others as this awakens the music of your life.

There can now be no automatic responses. They will be fresh, just like you.

Let every rule you've ever let

hold you back creatively

run a little ragged or loose

and then (lovingly even)

let go of the bunch

step back and spin

and spin again

and then: pick the first crooked line up,

dust it off, smile, and set it free, or

let it

go

in a

different direction.

JOY

THE
LIVING
GAME

Skeptic,
meet Splendid.
Curiosity,
meet
A Particular Joy.

After shopping at the market the other day, I arrived home with a trunk full of bags to unload. Happy to be home, my last chore of the day almost complete, I'd soon have time to unwind before starting dinner. As I began to unload everything into the kitchen, I could hear my daughter laughing outside. John was out back with Lulu, and they were bumping the volleyball back and forth.

"Mom, come play!" What an invitation. The sound of my daughter's voice and the whacking and bouncing of the ball: my beautiful life was calling.

But at first, my busy mind's immediate reaction was, *I have work to do,* and *I don't have time for this,* and *I need to start dinner.* But I remembered (and I told that busy mind of mine)—*I don't play that game anymore.*

I have learned to play the Living game instead of the Busy game.

I earned this lesson the hard way, through illness. And cultivating it has taken time and practice. But I do it now—seek these moments of joy—as if my life depends on it, because now I believe it does. And if I give in to my busy mind, it will steal these moments from me. Forever.

I hurriedly unpacked the frozen foods into the freezer and made my way outside for twenty minutes of liberating fun, bumping and batting the ball in a circle with my beloveds. Joy just seems to erupt sometimes when we least expect it.

How these moments in life open us up to living and show us our real treasure. We can feel our life, our bodies, our laughter, our vibrance.

Yes, joy just seems to erupt. And we should expect it more often and welcome it with enthusiasm. But also, we should create it. Joy has become a necessity for me, and I believe it is a necessity for all of us if we want to live healthy lives and affect others positively.

There are people in my life who have really figured out how to integrate this secret deep into their operating system. Some carry a quiet joy as a sister to the compassion they have gained in some way or another. They smile with their mouth and eyes. They are not uptight but instead move about with ease and playfulness. They drink joy from the moment and pour this presence back into the world—to all they encounter. I seek this way. It takes time. But I'm on the path.

Thinking back to the years before I got cancer, I wasn't living anywhere near real joy. The demands placed on me left me exhausted most of the time, eventually throwing me out of balance and making me sick.

I was performing my life, not truly living in it.

But it wasn't too late (it's never too late!) to get back to living. To let joy permeate through every hard place left in me. And though I still struggle, I try to live this way every day. I take joy wherever I can get it and set about to walk through my days in the wonder of it.

After our volleyball session, my family and I rolled back into the kitchen, where they helped me unload the rest of the groceries. I set a pot of water on the stove to boil and began chopping vegetables, with a full heart, in the pleasant fragrance of life, in the presence of my companions, in the expanse of joy.

AN INVITATION TO . . .

play

There are two main ways I've come to notice play in life.

There is the mind game—a competitive game we play with ourselves, where we habitually race to achieve whatever it is that we have determined will make us successful. This mind game typically makes us anxious, because we've been conditioned to play to achieve and win. Also because the object of the game keeps changing—there's always more we've yet to accomplish—we can never reach the goal.

And then there is the soul game—a fulfilling, noncompetitive practice. The only requirement here is that we show up for ourselves and court joy through the quality of our attentiveness and openness. There is no goal per se, and this game isn't about "winning." But it does have its rewards, the greatest of which is cultivating more presence in your life. This yields all kinds of crazy-good benefits and insights.

Some spectators of the mind game like to keep us there, as it serves their needs over our own. The soul game, however, seeks none of this outside approval. As such a self-enriching endeavor, it can feel a little rebellious. This is good! Accept this feeling as growth and normalize it.

Learn to sense the difference between this competitive mind game that we often play and the soul game, and choose to play the soul game every chance you get. Be enthusiastic, and don't hesitate. Your life (Joy!) awaits.

In Tiny We Trust
A semi manifesto

All hail the small, and beautiful.
We believe
In the evolution of memories
And unchanging, unapologetic love,
In being both lost, and found, and found again.
In writing your own way (and humbly asking for help),
In liberation, and joyous return
In seemingly impossible narratives made true,
In freedom, in family, in homecomings,
In recognizing treasure as the love in between
All of us
little points on a map, our lives and cherished
markers.

GET
THEE
TO THE
GREEN
WORLD

Scan the
landscape
a little longer
and soon
you'll see
yourself . . .

And now, with much gratitude, it is time for a breath of fresh air. To step into the ever-present antidote for anything that ails you and our most persistent, dependable, ongoing celebration: nature.

In Shakespeare's plays, issues get resolved when characters take a nature break. He sends them into the woods to distance themselves from the treacherous civilized world in order to glean some truth about themselves. In *As You Like It*, the bard writes about the treasure we find in nature: "This our life, exempt from public haunt, finds tongues in trees, books in the running brooks, sermons in stones, and good in everything."

Nature is awash in wonder and magic: abundant, healing, ever present, and always open. A life-giving, regenerative force of transformation, manifestation, and mystery. No "wonder" why the pastoral has such a persistent role in Shakespeare and why the natural world inspires art, music, prose, and poetry. Nature is very much who we are. Her sprawling leafy branches, waterways, and stones belong to us, and we to them. She beckons us from our oft-agitated lives to feel our insignificance and our power all at once, as she pulses with energy and pulses within us.

In the "tongues, books, and sermons" that Shakespeare speaks of in the quote above, there is a profound sense of wonder, and this wisdom: that these divine encounters are ours to have and that in nature we can find "good in everything."

To paraphrase Shakespeare again, in the words of *Macbeth*: We humans so often "fret our hour upon the stage." Life is fleeting and short. We shouldn't and needn't fret and waste time. We know this in our hearts, but in case we need some words, here is my stab at a Shakespearean-esque mantra, so we don't forget:

Get thee to the green world.

Because in the green world, we come alive in ourselves. I've experienced this healing so often that seeking nature has become essential. And it's a miracle how it works, each time, every time, without fail. When I walk alone on a trail, I feel the trees bow to me, and so you might see me bowing back to them. An incredible disappearance is enacted as my worldly concerns fall away and eventually dissolve, leaving me at peace. The outside chatter I brought with me slows down at first and then stops. A quiet cathedral now, a sense of wonder hangs in the air—a sense of timelessness.

Describing "me" in the green world is merely a reminder to get *thee* to the green world. And if you need a nudge, dear fellow actor, try this: Imagine your life as a play. And that the turning point in your current scene (or your day, your story, your life)—*the scene when things are set right*—can only happen when you leave the world of human foibles so that you may have a profound encounter with nature.

Please do it. Go there. Take your heart to the green world.

Wander in warm nights lit by golden summery moons and (always) magic. Embrace a tree or two while walking in the woods (or neighborhood park, garden, or your yard). Let yourself be moved by nature's myriad tiny miracles in motion.

And remember, you are also a miracle—a divine, natural part of all of this beauty.

connect with nature

When we are disconnected from the natural world, we can forget who we really are. We can't let this happen. There is just so much wonder and good living to be found within nature.

Within.

This word changes so much of our interpretation of the essence of nature. And existence.

Just as we breathe the air, the trees breathe it too. Pardon me—this is not meant to be morbid, but the opposite (and something to really remember): If you were to die on the trail, your body would eventually become plants' nutrients. You would be integrated into those same trees you may have bowed to on a transcendent stroll beneath them.

This is astounding! Your nature that exists within nature itself is astounding.

Take this in, and feel it. Do everything you can to maintain a connection to the natural world that you are so blessed to be a part of. It is in you and all around you. You are one and the same. Pure wonder.

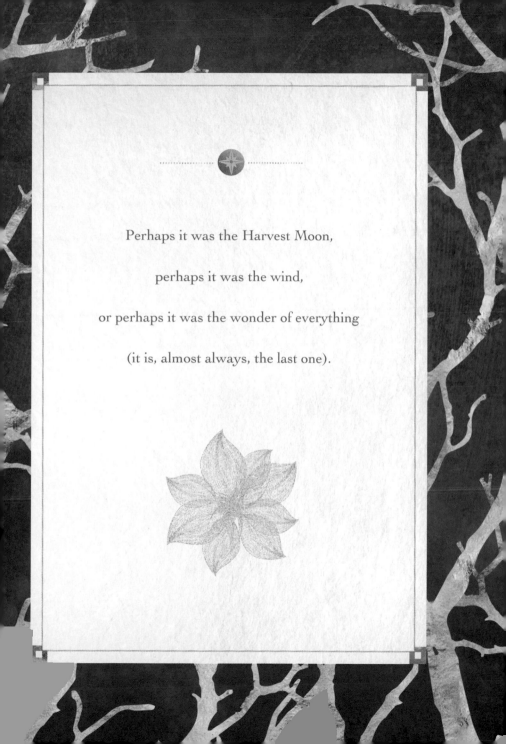

Perhaps it was the Harvest Moon,

perhaps it was the wind,

or perhaps it was the wonder of everything

(it is, almost always, the last one).

PERSONHOOD

AS YOU ARE, NOT AS YOU SHOULD BE

Encountering
the miraculous
is not a rare thing.
Noticing it is.
First step: notice that
YOU are part of it.

Every morning, I drink my cafe latte in a handmade ceramic mug. The same cup every day. A local ceramicist made it, and I chose it because of how it feels in my hand. First, there is its shape. Slightly curved, with a handle that is big enough to slip my first three fingers through it, pinky below the handle, thumb resting alongside the lip. The mug is partially dip-glazed in several blues that layer together—the underglaze is the color of a robin's egg, and then on top of that is a French blue that spills down the inside and outside of the mug from the top, interacting with the color underneath. At the bottom of the mug—the part that was not dipped—is the raw clay, an earthen brown that's rough to the touch compared with the smooth glazes.

Each morning, as I do my ritualistic "mug hug," I meditate. I hold the mug with my right hand, feeling the smooth glaze on the handle side. Then I cup it with my left hand and trace the diagonal edge of the glaze, holding on to the warmth of the raw clay, running my thumb along its rough surface. I love both aspects of the mug—the artfully applied, beautiful blue glazes and the exposed naked clay. I don't know how to truly describe the magic in this clay wonder, but it helps me drink my coffee mindfully, and I love that. I feel the mug in my hands and the artist at work. I feel connected somehow, and it feels authentic.

I look forward to this mug every morning. It has a beautiful energy and form that can't be replicated. And just as there is a difference between mass-produced goods and handmade ones, there is a difference between an authentically lived life and a superficial one.

So often in life, we follow paths we thought would lead us where we need to go. But then we awaken one day and don't recognize ourselves, instead being led further away from who we truly are. This is everything. Are we pursuing a deeper relationship with ourselves in our precious days here, or are we on someone else's path instead?

Or, to put it another way: What life are you looking for?

And what if you are already there?

And if you are there, are you living it authentically?

Like how the glaze on my mug honors the clay, we are to honor the wild energies that were placed inside of us if we are to live at all. These signature energies are the animating force in the clay of who we are. We each received this gift when we were born. Full of boundless possibilities, it is up to each of us to come alive, in authentic form—to choose what's real. To choose love, first for ourselves: in our raw, rough, unpolished, very real, and very beautiful selves.

Growth into your authentic self takes allowing and accepting a life that isn't "out there" but that is close by.

Your own wondrous life.

The authenticity that seeks you only requires that you be liberated into nothing else but the life that is yours and only yours.

When you live in your authenticity, you discover the great freedom to love yourself as you are, not as you should be. And this contribution to all: to love another as they are, not as they should be.

celebrate yourself

Through the lens of wonder, see yourself. Beauty from all angles.

You at your most authentic: an original work in progress. That glow, the truth of you, your light. It comforts, reveals, augments, and transforms . . . everything. It stuns us with its power. It is the splendor of your being, of self-liberation, that liberates us.

You have so much life-giving light within you. The world needs that precious resource. *We need your light.* Cast that glow right where you are. Let the wonder of it reveal possibility. Let your mind and body come together. Let it create a oneness that outshines any limits or fears.

Celebrate this: the moment you knew, found, saw, realized, witnessed, experienced revelation or transformation, or simply your own personal EUREKA. And if you're waiting for that to happen, be reminded: You are the channel (and it is happening right here, at this moment, in every moment).

Rise and reveal

your bright self

Part of the perfect, miraculous now

Integral, ascendent, starlike, and shining—

Embroidered in all stories, all lyrics, all fables

Elemental and extraordinary

you are evidence of wonder.

EACH OTHER

OUR PRECIOUS, HIDDEN VALUES

Wonder lights us up,
incandescently so,
a chorus of
glowing-heart balloons
floating over the sea . . .

We are infinitely more than what we believe about ourselves. And we have infinitely more possibilities available to us than we think we do.

Consider our collective origin. Science tells us that everything, including all of us, is made from the dust and bits of long-ago and faraway stars. What a dazzling and overwhelmingly bombastic entry point for life! The idea that people are created from celestial fragments is pretty divine, both literally and figuratively.

Pause a moment.

Regardless of where we came from, who our parents are, where we grew up, how blessed we were, or how we may have struggled: we are all from the same golden, glowing, otherworldly, gorgeous, transformative moment.

Imagine that.

Now think about a few things that you believe about yourself. Maybe it's your gender, nationality, political beliefs, familial roles, or religious affiliation. Whether you are fit or not, overweight or not. Funny/smart/hardworking/kind/successful or not. If "human" was not one of your belief thoughts, don't fret. We have all been conditioned to identify as something "more" than our most common denominator (even if that "more" is something negative or unfitting). This is what makes us "special," but it is also the thing that the media and those in power use to separate us from each other.

But the thing is, you are so much more than whatever image you have of yourself. We are so much more than the images we have of each other.

After all: we are each from the same transformative moments.

And in a way, because of this, aren't we all a little more dazzling, a little closer to our faraway former starlight selves than we might immediately think?

This is a wonderful cosmic truth. We are all more dazzling than we are able to let on. But we are so roped into a system of outward identity and achievement, we sometimes forget that we can look beyond this image to seek a deeper sense of self in each other. We sometimes forget that there is a connective thread of divinity woven through our hearts and the hearts of others.

The course of our lives can change entirely, beautifully, and boldly by the simplest action. Recognizing that we are each a miracle is a good start. If we can navigate with our sense of wonder more regularly, it will be much easier to recognize our starry selves in each other. When we do, we find each other again and again. We share stories. We make meaning together. We celebrate the small and large. We do not give up, because while we might all be on slightly different personal journeys, we are also intersecting one another on an infinite path of journeying itself. And tasked with the challenges on this Earth, we can give each other great strength and purpose.

If and when we take the time to notice each other's hidden, precious values, we each glow a little brighter, and nothing is impossible.

love one another

A reminder if anyone has forgotten: We are all, each of us, and every material thing in the entire world (even things we haven't found yet), made of bits and pieces of starry minutiae, broken apart and exploded and transformed into new and wonderful things long ago. And we are transforming still.

Our lives as humans from this same origin are greatly improved when we share our journeys with a benevolent heart. When, in both interior and tangible ways, we encourage each other to lift our various unique and beautiful spirits.

Practice understanding another in their particular circumstances. Because although we share some starry history, we are all going through something different. Do your best at this. Give your attention, wisdom, and time—and receive back connection and life.

Carry on in kindness. Create a story of belonging that other travelers can tell at a later time, in their own way, with familiar meaning and precious effect.

See love as the most reasonable action. Always.

We are all

Blazing stars

All of us

Each of us

All the time

Twinkling onward

We are the little lighthouses

Guiding each other toward safety

We are the lucky feathers

We are the fireflies

We are the glimmering things that

Brighten and enchant

We are the ones that save each other.

With wide-open eyes
and wider-opened hearts,
remember, Dear One:
We are here to change
and be changed
by the world,
by will, and by *wonder.*

AN INVITATION TO KEEP GOING

The old movie stops with THE END on the screen, but don't we all agree that in some way, it's never really over? That the story might stop but life keeps going—the story changed you, and in experiencing it, you changed the story.

An epilogue sets up part two, or two thousand, but by itself, as a thing, it does little more than set up.

This is where you come in.

This, fellow travelers, is an invitation to keep going—and so I invite you, please: take these stories, poems, learnings, leanings, and insights and make them into something unanticipated, but equally or more important.

Keep living, shifting to, and sharing the way of wonder: because in doing so, you help rewrite the world.

ABOUT THE AUTHORS

PATTI PAGLIEI and JOHN SIMPSON are a husband-and-wife duo and partners in a creative syndicate that includes the inspirational jewelry brand Waxing Poetic. Their life together has been alighted to the way of wonder through their adventures and artful endeavors, but also several life-changing health, home, and business challenges. Forced to reexamine their perceived limitations, they uncovered the way for this book, which they consider—along with their family and zest for life—one of their greatest successes. They currently live in Santa Barbara, California, with their daughter, Lulu.

To connect with John and Patti, head over to www.johnandpatti.com and on Instagram @johnandpatti.

To check out Waxing Poetic jewelry, please visit www.waxingpoetic.com and on Instagram @waxingpoetic.

ACKNOWLEDGMENTS

We are deeply grateful to b, whose heart and poetry have made this book possible (and whose real name shall remain a mystery, because: wonder). You have taught us so much about life and writing. Your words are everything.

Ceaseless love and gratitude go out to Patti's sister, Lizanne Hales, whose support of the dream of this book helped make it real. To everyone at Waxing Poetic and The Shopkeepers: Thanks for keeping things going so that we could get this work done. You are not just coworkers but also friends.

We would like to thank our friend Kyra Thompson for her wisdom and spirit. To our incredible daughter Lulu, for sharing her story of courage (and for making her own mac 'n' cheese and other dinners while we worked). And to our family and friends, who are with us in all of our stories.

Thank you to our publisher, Rage Kindelsperger, who gave us the brilliant invitation to write a book about wonder—a gift of a lifetime. Big gratitude to Keyla Pizarro-Hernández, whose thoughtful editing brought the best of this book to light; and to our agent, Adriann Zurhellen—we are grateful for your guidance. Each of you has been such a pleasure to work with.

One last thanks to our fortunes—good and bad—for astonishing us and giving us a life of wonder. To wonder itself, which has shown us the way. To you, for journeying with us.

This book is offered in dedication to Patti's mom, Rita. You teach us all to live.

REFERENCES

Hooks, Bell. *All about Love: New Visions*. Harper, an imprint of HarperCollins Publishers, 2000.

Ikemoto, Takashi, and Lucien 1924- Stryk. *Zen Poetry: Let the Spring Breeze Enter*. Grove Press, 1995.

Oxford English Dictionary, https://www.oed.com/.

Shakespeare, William, and O. J. Stevenson. *Shakespeare's As You like It*. Copp, Clark, 1919.

Shakespeare, William. *Macbeth*. Oxford: Oxford University Press, 1623.

Thoreau, Henry David. *Journal*, 5 July 1851.

Turner, Elizabeth Hutton, et al. *Georgia O'Keeffe: The Poetry of Things*. Phillips Collection, 1999.

Williams, Tennessee, and Kate Walker. *The Glass Menagerie*. New Directions, 2019.

First published in 2023 by Rock Point,
an imprint of The Quarto Group,
142 West 36th Street, 4th Floor,
New York, NY 10018, USA
T (212) 779-4972 F (212) 779-6058
www.Quarto.com

Rock Point titles are also available at discount
for retail, wholesale, promotional, and bulk
purchase. For details, contact the Special Sales
Manager by email at specialsales@quarto.com
or by mail at The Quarto Group,
Attn: Special Sales Manager,
100 Cummings Center Suite 265D,
Beverly, MA 01915 USA.

10 9 8 7 6 5 4 3 2 1

ISBN: 978-1-63106-962-8

Library of Congress Cataloging-in-Publication
Data

Names: Pagliei, Patti, author. | Simpson, John
  (Entrepreneur), author.
Title: The way of wonder : invitations and
simple practices for a vibrant life/
  Patti Pagliei and John Simpson.
Description: New York, NY : Rock Point, 2023.
  | Includes bibliographical references. |
  Summary: "Find your way into the wonder
  of everyday and live a life full of nows with
  the powerful advice in The Way of Wonder"--
  Provided by publisher.
Identifiers: LCCN 2023005030 (print) | LCCN
  2023005031 (ebook) | ISBN 9781631069628
  (hardcover) | ISBN 9780760383995 (ebook)
Subjects: LCSH: Wonder. | Self-realization. |
  Conduct of life.
Classification: LCC BF575.A9 P34 2023 (print)
  | LCC BF575.A9 (ebook) | DDC 155.2--dc23
  eng/20230202
LC record available at https://lccn.loc
  gov/2023005030
LC ebook record available at https://lccn.loc
  gov/2023005031

Publisher: Rage Kindelsperger
Editorial Director: Erin Canning
Creative Director: Laura Drew
Managing Editor: Cara Donaldson
Editor: Keyla Pizarro-Hernández
Cover and Interior Design: Marisa Kwek
Page Layout: Tara Long

Printed in China

This book provides general information on various widely known concepts and widely accepted
images that tend to evoke feelings of strength and confidence. However, it should not be relied
upon as recommending or promoting any specific diagnosis or method of treatment for a particular
condition, and it is not intended as a substitute for medical advice or for direct diagnosis and
treatment of a medical condition by a qualified physician. Readers who have questions about a
particular condition, possible treatments for that condition, or possible reactions from the condition
or its treatment should consult a physician or other qualified healthcare professional.

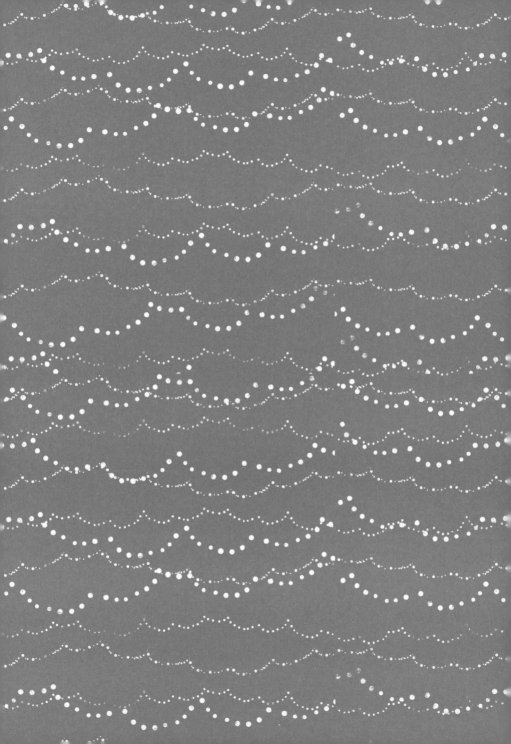